श्री:

Śree Lalitā Trishatee

(300 divine names of the celestial mother –
with meanings and commentaries)

*

Dr. Ramamurthy N

M.Sc., B.G.L., CAIIB, CCP, DSADP, CISA, PMP, CGBL, 6σ–Black–Belt, Ph.D.

*

Name of the Book: *Śree Lalitā Trishatee*
(300 divine names of the celestial mother – with meanings and commentaries)

First Edition: 2013
Second Edition: 2016
Third Edition: 2025

Author: Dr. Ramamurthy N, Chennai.
http://ramamurthy.jaagruti.co.in/

ISBN: 978-93-82237-17-4

No of pages: 165

*****

TABLE OF CONTENTS

Dedication....4

Foreword....5

Introduction....7

Śrī Lalitā Triśatī....10

पूर्व भाग: *Pūrva Bhāgaḥ* (Beginning Part)....18

Śrī Lalitā Triśatī Japa Vidhānam....25

Śrīmad Vāgbhava Kūṭam – श्रीमद्वाग्भवकूटम्....31

Madhyakūṭam – मध्यकूटम्....69

Śaktikūṭam – शक्तिकूटम्....103

उत्तर भाग: *Uttara Bhāgaḥ* (End part)....125

Annexure 1....140

Annexure 2....152

About the Author....163

Bibiliography....165

*****

Dedication

Mātru Devo Bhava

I dedicate this book with *pranāms* to my mother *Śrīmati* **Alankāravalli Ammal**, who brought me to this level right from scratch. She is the Divine Mother *Śrī Devī* in the human form in this world. Though she is not physically available to see me at this glassy, I am sure all these are possible only with her blessings and she continues to live with me spiritually.

Dr. Ramamurthy N

*****

SWAMI RAMANANDA SARASWATI
Srichakra Rajarajeswari Peetam
No: D-5 / New No.14, Rajam Road, (Opp.Nalampuri Vinayagar Temple),
T.V.S. Nagar, Madurai-625 003, Ph : 88709 44696

Foreword

15th May 2013

Among the *Śanmata* established by *Śrī Ādi Śaṇkara, Śākta* worship is the best and

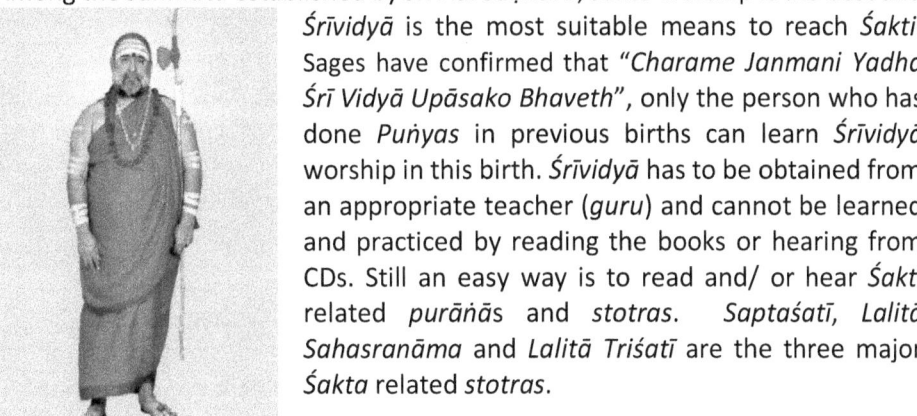

Śrīvidyā is the most suitable means to reach *Śakti*. Sages have confirmed that *"Charame Janmani Yadha Śrī Vidyā Upāsako Bhaveth"*, only the person who has done *Puṅyas* in previous births can learn *Śrīvidyā* worship in this birth. *Śrīvidyā* has to be obtained from an appropriate teacher (*guru*) and cannot be learned and practiced by reading the books or hearing from CDs. Still an easy way is to read and/ or hear *Śakti* related *purāṅā*s and *stotras*. *Saptaśatī, Lalitā Sahasranāma* and *Lalitā Triśatī* are the three major *Śakta* related *stotras*.

There is a general feeling that *Śrī Lalitā Triśatī* is difficult to chant or read. But it is not really so. Out of the three *stotras Śrī Lalitā Triśatī* is the most sacred and result oriented, since It is *Sarva Poorthikara Stotram*. Also, it encompasses *Pancadaśākşarī mantra* Itself in it. As detailed in the results part by the author, reading or chanting or simply hearing this *Stotra* or performing *Archana* using the 300 divine names will fetch enormous results as desired by the devotees. But still the results will be multiplied and also the errors or mistakes will be reduced If it is done after understanding the meaning of the names – not only the apparent meaning, but the inner meaning or *tattvas* represented by each name. Another benefit is – understanding the meanings would enable the worshippers to focus more on *Śrī Devī* and meditate upon **Her**.

In this regard this book will definitely be of use to the readers and *Śakta* worshippers. It is a good Idea that the author has given the names in Samskrutam also so that there would not be any mistake in pronouncing the names.

All the *Śrīvidyā* mantras are to be treated as very secret. It has been mentioned by the learned that a *Śrīvidyā* worshipper (*upāsaka*) should not reveal to all that he is a *Śrīvidyā* worshipper. More so the *mantras*. Even the *guru* should not teach the *mantras* to his disciples unless it is demanded by the disciple himself. This has been clearly explained in this book during the introduction part as a dialogue between Lord Hayagreeva and sage Agastya.

Śrī **Ramamurthy** is a seasoned and versatile personality in various fields. From the book his knowledge in Samskrutam can easily be understood. He has lot of passion for learning and equally spreading the knowledge as well. He has taken much effort to make the language so simple so that the book is understandable even by lay men. After reading this book in English we requested him to write the same book in Tamil also so that it could reach a wider public and immediately he responded and we have decided to publish the same.

We pray to *Śrī Devī*, to bestow her complete compassion on *Śrī* Ramamurthy to continue his service to the spirituality for a long time.

There is no doubt that *Śrī Devī* will shower her blessings to all the readers.

Nārāyana *Nārāyana* *Nārāyana*

With great love

Madurai
15th May 2013

*Śrī Rāmananda Saraswa*ti *Swam*i
Śrichakra Rajarajeswari Peeṭam

*****

श्री:

Introduction

ॐ – *Oṃ*

वन्दे विघ्नेश्वरं देवं सर्वसिद्धि प्रदायिनम् ।
वामाङ्करूढ वामाक्षी करपल्लव पूजितम् ॥ ॐ विघ्नेश्वराय नम: ॥
गुरुर्ब्रह्मा गुरुर्विष्णु: गुरुर्देवो महेश्वर: ।
गुरुस्साक्षात् परम् ब्रह्म तस्मै श्रीगुरवे नम: ॥ श्रीगुरुमूर्तये नम: ॥

Ṣanmata;

Hinduism is conglomeration of six different religions (or sub–religions) called *Ṣaṇmata*. This has been founded by *Śrī Ādi Śaṇkara* in the 8th Century C.E. It centers on the worship of the six main deities, viz, *Śiva, Viśṇu, Śakti, Gaṇeśa, Soorya* and *Skanda*. The sub–religions are called as;

- *Śaiva*, who mainly worship *Śiva*
- *Vaiṣṇava*, who mainly worship *Viṣṇu*
- *Śākta*, who mainly worship *Śakti*
- *Gāṇapatya*, who mainly worship *Gaṇapati* or *Gaṇeśa*
- *Soura*, who mainly worship *Sūrya* (the Sun God) and
- *Koumāra*, mainly who worship *Kumāra* or *Skanda*

This system is based on the belief in the essential oneness of all deities, the unity of Godhead and their conceptualisation of the myriad deities, as various manifestations of the one divine power, *Brahmam*. The above list does not include a sub–religion called *Smārtha* – generally understood as *Śaiva*. But *Smārtha* is a little different from *Śaiva*. They are *Sama–artha* – equally treating all the deities.

Śākta Religion;

The ardent devotees or worshippers of *Śakti* or *Śrī Devī* belong to *Śākta* religion. Among the various texts on *Śākta* the major ones are;

- The *Lalitā Sahasranāma* and *Lalitā Triśatī* – both contained in *Brahmāṇḍa Purāṇa* expound *Śrī Vidyā*. *Bhāskara Rāya*'s *Soubhāgya Bhāskaram* is a *Bhāshyam* (commentary) on *Lalitā Sahasranāma*.
- *Mārkaṇḍeya Purāṇa* contains in itself *Devī Mahātmya* also called as *Saptaśatī* (since it contains 700 verses – *Sapta* – 7 and *śatī* = 100). *Devī Bhāgavata* describes *Maṇidvīpa*, which is *Śrī Devī*'s abode.
- *Soundaryalaharī*, Sung by *Śrī Ādi Śaṇkara* describes *Śrī Devī's* beauty and used in many places to worship Her.

Śrī Ādi Śaṇkara, who himself is considered as an incarnation of Lord *Śiva* wrote *Bhashyam* to *Lalitā Triśatī*. Both *Lalitā Sahasranāma* and *Lalitā Triśatī* are in the hymn form of *Pancadaśī Mantra*. The verses in the hymns are split into 300 or 1000 names as the case may be.

Some other texts based on *Śākta* are – *Śrī Sūkta, Tripura Tāpini Upanishad, Prapanca Sāra Tantra, Kāmakalā Vilāsa, Tantrarāja Tantra, Tripurārṇava Tantra, Śrī Vidyārṇava Tantra, Jnānārnava Tantra, Dakshiṇāmūrti Samhita, Gāndharva Tantra, Nityā Śoḍaśikārnava, Yoginī Hrudaya* and so on.

Nāmāvalīs;

Archana or *Nāmāvalī* is performed on various Gods with *Aşţothra* (108), *Triśatī* (300) and *Sahasranāma* (1000) names. The *Sahasranāma* is repeated to count to Lakh or Koti, etc.

Lord *Śiva* is worshipped with *Triśatī Archana* through *Rudraprashna* and *Śrī Devee* through *Lalitā Triśatī* – *Śiva–Śakt*i equivalence.

According to *Śiva Purana "Avanarulāleye Avan Tāl Vanangi"* – to worship his feet with his own blessings – a humble attempt has been made in this book to provide in simple English the commentaries of the "*Lalitā Triśatī*". The English language cannot bring out the exact and complete sense (meaning) of many Samskruta words. The philosophical concepts expressed in Samskruta are so deep and often so complex; that the purports are more to be felt and intellectually and spiritually realised, than expressed in mere words. Many of the concepts are culture related and only a person born and brought up with interest in *Vedas* or is fully exposed to *Vedic* culture can fully comprehend the meanings. The extraordinary plasticity of the Samskruta language and often the multiplicity of the meanings of the Samskruta words and the possibility of changes in the meanings by slight alteration in the prefixes and/ or suffixes and the possibility of splitting complex words in different ways resulting in rendering different meanings of the compound words make Samskruta a unique language. These factors make it almost impossible to bring out in English, the exact force of the descriptions in Samskruta since the Samskruta words refer to psychological, spiritual and cultural concepts more than the dictionary meanings. These difficulties in expressing the concepts of the *Vedic* Sages in the English language necessitate repetitions – which may be sometimes boring, but which could not be avoided. With all these constraints an attempt has been made to bring out the commentaries of "*Lalitā Triśatī*" as much as possible simple English.

This author has earlier written a book "*Śrī Lalitā Sahasranāmam*" – a complete *Bāskararāya's Bhāshyam* in simple English. There were some requests to write a similar book *Lalitā Triśatī* in English and hence this book. This is mainly based on *Śrī Ādi Śaṇkara*'s commentaries on *Lalitā Triśatī*. Wherever possible comparison with *Lalitā Sahasranāma* and other texts are quoted. *Lalitā Sahasranāma*, wherever quoted is completely based on *Śrī* Bhāskararāya's commentaries. Hope the readers would be benefitted by reading this book and blessed by *Śrī Devī*.

Conventions used in this book; Wherever she is used to indicate *Śrī Devī* It has been written in bold as **She**. The transliterated Samskruta words are written in Italics – for instance *Devī*. When Samskruta words are transliterated in English diacritical marks are used to correctly pronounce the words. However, the same has not been used in its entirety in this book, since it makes the reading a little more difficult and since this book is intended for common audience.

My humble *pranāms* to HH *Śrī Rāmānanda Saraswa*ti *Swāmiji* of *Śrichakra Rājarājeswari Peeṭam,* Madurai for his nice introduction and some pleasantries about this edition and about me. I am more honoured. As ordained by him I have wrltten this book in Tamil also and the same has been published and released by him during Vy*ā*sa Poornima in July 2013.

Sincere thanks are due to all those who supported in this noble cause. The readers are requested to give all comments and feedback to the author.

Oṃ Tat Sat

Chennai
August 2013

Ramamurthy N

*****

श्रीः

Śrī Gurubhyo Namaḥ
Śrī Lalitā Mahatripura Sundaryai Namaḥ

Śrī Lalitā Triśatī

Among the 18 main *puranas*, written by Veda Vyas, *Brahmāṇḍa Purāṅa* is well known for the extolling of *Lalitā*. It explains in detail the appearance of the Goddess *Lalitā* to save the world from the clutches of the demon *Bhanḍāsura*. There are three important sub–texts in this *purana*.

The first one is *Lalitopākhyāna*, consisting of 45 chapters and is found in the last section of the *purāṅa*. The last five chapters are especially exalting the Divine mother, explain the significance of the *mantra* of the goddess (*Śoḍaśākşarī*), the various *mudras* and postures to be practiced, meditations, initiations etc. and the mystical placement of the deities involved in *Śrī Chakra*.

The second text is the celebrated *Lalitā Sahasranāma*, which consists of 320 verses in three chapters.

The third text is the *Lalitā Triśatī* in which 300 names of *Śrī Devī* are featured. This *Triśatī* is also called as *Sarva Pūrthikara Stotram* – which means a hymn that can satiate any wish completely. There is a well–known commentary on this work attributed to *Śrī Ādi Shankarācārya*.

Lalitā Triśatī and *Lalitā Sahasranāma* are in the form of dialogue between the sage Agastya and Lord Hayagreeva. Hayagreeva is an incarnation of Lord *Vişŋu* assuming the form of a horse to kill a demon by the same name. Agastya was a sage of great renown, who is immortalised as a star in the celestial heavens (one of the seven *Rishi*–s – *saptarishi* or Ursa Major). He is the patron saint of Tamilnadu being of a founder of a system of medicine called Siddha and also having drunk the River Ganga in his *kamandalu*. According to Yāska's *Nirukta*, Agastya is the half–brother of the great sage, *Vashishta*.

The story of the meeting of Agastya and Hayagreeva is explained in *Lalitopākhyāna* and is quite interesting. Agastya was visiting several places of pilgrimage and was sad to see many people steeped in ignorance and involved in only sensual pleasures. He came to Kancheepuram and worshiped Kamakshi and sought a solution for the masses. Pleased with the devotion and his concern for the society, Lord *Vişŋu* appeared before him and provided with the solution of 'curing' the worldly folk from ignorance. He explained that He is the primordial principle and the source and the end of everything.

Though **He** is above forms and *guṇās*, He involves himself in them. He goes on to explain that a person should recognise that He is the *pradhāna* (primordial)

transformed into the universe and that He is also the *purusha* (conscious spirit) who is transcendental and beyond all qualities (*guṇa*–s) and forms. However, to recognise this, one has to perform severe penance, self–discipline etc. Since this is difficult for an ordinary human being, Lord *Viṣŋu* advised that the worship of *Śrī Devī* will achieve the purpose of life, given as liberation from bondage, very easily. He pointed out that even other Gods like *Śiva* and Brahma have worshiped *Śrī Devī*. He concluded his discourse saying that this was revealed to Agastya so that he (Agastya) can spread the message to gods, sages and humans. *Viṣŋu* suggested Agastya to approach his incarnation, Hayagreeva and disappeared from Agastya's sight.

Agastya approached Hayagreeva with devotion and reverence. Hayagreeva reveals to Agastya that the great *Śrī Devī* is without beginning or end and is the foundation of the entire universe. The great *Devee* abides in everyone and can be realised only through meditation. The worship of Her is done with the *Lalitā Sahasranāma* (1000 names) and Hayagreeva taught him the great *Sahasranāma* verses.

After this Agastya thanked Hayagreeva and told him that though he has heard about *Śrī Chakra Upasana* and the *Sahasranāma* he has a feeling of lacking in satisfaction of knowing all the secrets and caught hold of Hayagreeva' s feet. Hayagreeva was taken aback and kept quiet. At that time *Śrī Devī* appeared before Hayagreeva and told him that both Agastya and his wife Lopāmudra are very dear to her and that Agastya is worthy of receiving the most secret *Lalitā Triśatī* and then disappeared. Hayagreeva lifted up Agastya and told him that he is indeed a great man since *Śrī Devī* herself had commanded him to impart the *Triśatī* to Agastya.

He also told him that he was fortunate to have Agastya as a disciple since he had the vision of *Lalitā* due to Agastya. He then gave him the following *Triśatī*[1].

The *Lalitā Triśatī* gives three hundred names of *Lalitā*, just as *Lalitā Sahasranāma* is a compendium of 1,000 names for the mother goddess. This Triśatī is considered to be even more sacred and powerful than the *Sahasranāma*. The names are not just names, each one of them is a *mantra* – in the sense that they have impenetrable spiritual meanings and when recited, the very recitation, even without the understanding of the meaning, can give powerful effects, just because of the vibrations they can generate. Every *sahasranāma* and every name of God has this characteristic, but in the case of *Lalitā Triśatī*, it is expressly certified to be so. Consequently, each name is dense with meanings, not only with the obvious ones but with several non–obvious profound interpretations. The best source for the meanings of the names in *Triśatī* is *Śrī Ādi Sankara* who has written an elaborate commentary on it.

There is a fifteen–letter *mantra* for the Goddess which is not only famous but at the same time forms the greatest of secrets in the worship of the Goddess – secret in the sense that the *mantra* has to be learned from a *guru* orally after a number of pre–requisites are fulfilled to the satisfaction of the *guru*. The three hundred names in the *Triśatī* occur in groups of twenty names, one for each letter of the fifteen–letter *mantra* (*Pancadaśākṣarī*). Hence the;

- First Group – *Śrīmadvāgbhavakūṭam* – श्रीमद्वाग्भवकूटम्
  - First 20 names all start with the letter '*ka*–क' which is the first letter of the *mantra*.
  - Second 20 names start with '*e*–ए' – the 2nd letter of the *mantra*
  - Third 20 names start with '*ee*–ई' – the 3rd letter of the *mantra*
  - Fourth 20 names start with '*la*–ल' – the 4th letter of the *mantra*
  - Fifth 20 names start with '*Hrīm*–ह्रीम्' – the 5th letter of the *mantra*

---

[1] There is a mandate to all the *gurus* (teachers) that these texts like *Lalitā Shasranāma, Lalitā Trishatee, Shreevidyā mantras*, etc., are all very secret. These texts should not be taught to any disciple unless the disciple is examined to be fit to learn and also the disciple himself asks the *Guru* to teach him. The same author has earlier written a book "Power of *Shree Vidyā*", which details more on these aspects.

- The face of *Śrī Devī* represents the first portion of *Pancadaśākşarī Mantra* consisting of the above five letters.

- Second Group – *Madhyakūṭam* – मध्यकूटम्
  - Sixth 20 names start with *'ha*–ह' – the 6th letter of the *mantra*
  - Seventh 20 names start with '*sa*–स' – the 7th letter of the *mantra*
  - Eighth 20 names start with '*ka*–क' – the 8th letter of the *mantra*
  - Ninth 20 names start with '*ha*–ह' – the 9th letter of the *mantra*
  - Tenth 20 names start with '*la*–ल' – the 10th letter of the *mantra*
  - Eleventh 20 names start with *'Hrīm*– ह्रीम् – the 11th letter of the *mantra*
- The part of *Śrī Devī*'s body below the neck and above the hip represents the central portion of *Pancadaśākşarī Mantra* consisting of the above six letters.

- Third Group – *Śaktikūṭam* – शक्तिकूटम्
  - Twelfth 20 names start with '*sa*–स' – the 12th letter of the *mantra*
  - Thirteenth 20 names start with '*ka*–क' – the 13th letter of the *mantra*
  - Fourteenth 20 names start with '*la*–ल' – the 14th letter of the *mantra*
  - Fifteenth 20 names start with *'Hrīm*–ह्रीम्' – the 15th letter of the *mantra*
- The part of *Śrī Devī*'s body below the hip represents the bottom portion of *Pancadaśākşarī Mantra* consisting of the above four letters.

An analysis of the names reveals that all the 300 names in this *Triśatī* start only with 7 letters. The below table gives more analysis:

Starting Letter	**Names** From **– To**	**Number of names**
Ka – क	1 to 20, 141 to 160 and 241 to 260	60
E – ए	21 to 40	20
Ee – ई	41 to 60	20
La – ल	61 to 80, 181 to 200 and 261–280	60
Hrīm – ह्रीम्	81 to 100, 201 to 220 and 281–300	60
ha – ह	101 to 120 and 161 to 180	40
Sa – स	121 to 140 and 221 to 240	40
	Total	300

in this regard the following names of *Śrī Devī*, same as the names of the above groups in the same order, from *Śrī Lalitā Sahsranāma* is worth noting;

- 85th name – *Śrīmad Vāgbhava Kūṭaika Svarūpa Mukhapamkajā* – श्रीमद्वाग्भवकूटैक स्वरूपमुखपंकजा
- 86th name – *Kaṇṭhādhaḥ Kaṭiparyanta Madhya Kūṭa Svarūpiṇī* – कण्ठाध: कटिपर्यन्तमध्यकूटस्वरूपिणी
- 87th name – *Śaktikūṭaika Tāpanna Kaṭyadho Bhāga Dhāriṇī* – शक्तिकूटैकतापन्नकट्यधोभागधारिणी

The *'Mantra'* is, therefore, in a coded form with very deep meaning for each alphabet. The code has been explained by *Śrī Ādi Sankara* in his *Soundaryalaharī* (32nd verse) as;

शिव: शक्ति: काम: क्षितिरथ रवि: शीतकिरण: स्मरो हंस: शक्रस्तदनु च परामारहरय: ।
अमी हृल्लेखाभि–स्तिसृभि–रवसानेषु घटिता भजन्ते वर्णास्ते तव जननि नामावयवताम् ॥

Śivaḥ Śaktiḥ Kāmaḥ Kşitiratha Raviḥ Śītakiranaḥ
Smaro Hamsaḥ Śakrastadanu Ca Parāmāraharayaḥ I
Amī Hrullekhābhi-Stisrubhi-Ravasāneśu Ghaṭitā
Bhajante Varnāste Tava Janani Nāmāvayavatām II

Oh Mother! The root alphabets:

- *ka*–क pertains to *Śiva*
- *e*–ए relates *Shak*ti
- *ee*–ई relates *Kāma* or *Manmata* (Cupid)
- *la*–ल relates Earth
- *ha*–ह relates Sun
- *sa*–स relates Moon, who has cool rays
- *ka*–क relates *Kāma* or *Manmata* (Cupid)
- *ha*–ह, contained in the *Hamsa mantra*, relates Ether
- *la*–ल relates *Indra*
- *sa*–स relates *Parā*
- *ka*–क relates *Kāma* or *Manmata* (Cupid)
- *la*–ल relates *Hari*

These alphabets or syllables, when conjoined severally at their ends with three *Hrillekhas* (three main tasks creation, protection and destruction) become the components of thy name. The above verse deals with the 15 letters of *Pancadaśākşarī mantra*. Hence the repeated letters are mentioned separately. Also, the same letter relates differently depending on its place in the *Pancadaśākşarī mantra*.

This verse of *Soundaryalaharī* indirectly gives the most holy *Pancha-dashākşarī mantra*, which consists of three parts viz., *ka–ā–ee–la–Hrīm* as *Vāgbhavakūta, ha – sa–ka–ha – la–Hrīm* as *Kāmarājakūta* and *sa–ka–la–Hrīm* as *Shaktikūta*. These parts are respectively called *Vahni Kundalini, Soorya Kundalini* and *Soma kundalini*.

The *mantra* is thus well–known because the text of the *mantra* can be guessed by putting together the first letters of the fifteen groups of 20 names. But no one is not supposed to be in possession of the *mantra* until it has been 'got' from a *guru* – who must have himself repeatedly recited it several thousands of times (minimum of 15 lakhs times – *Akshara Laksha* – since this *mantra* has 15 letters) with all the reverence and concentration it demands so that he possesses the spirit of the *mantra* in him.

This concept of the spiritual possession of a *mantra* is an important part of the culture of Hindu religion. The necessity to repeat the *mantra* has an extraordinary emphasis because the effect of the *mantra* is held to be proportional to the intensity of the spiritual possession of it and this latter, is directly proportional to the number of times it has been repeated formally and reverentially.

But the *Upanishads* speak of Her as "the Witness, the Pure Sentience and the Attribute-less". The *Sahasranāma* itself includes the name *Nirguna*, the attribute-less. in spite of all this the attribute-less Absolute is here talked of as possessing attributes. They are actually attributes superimposed on *Śrī Devī*, who is the *Chit sha*kti, the Consciousness Absolute. The attributes themselves are only adjuncts and what we are praising is only the Absolute seen through these adjuncts. There is nothing wrong in worshipping the mother in this attributed form rather than in the attribute-less way. Thus worshipped, *Śrī Devī* will grace us to become capable of transcending the abyss of plurality and comprehend Her as the Formless Absolute.

It can be noted that *Triśatī* describes in details about the formation of *Śrī Chakra* and its parts[2] – which are integrated and mingled with each other.

This Triśatī consists of;

1. *Poorva peetikā* or *bhāga* – 29 verses
2. *Nyāsa* – method of meditation
3. *Stotra*/ hymn – 59 verses, which are split into 300 names
4. *Uttara Peetikā* or *bhāga* – *Phalashruti* – 58.5 verses – it may be noted the results or fruits are given in number of verses equal to the Stotra. The results are equal or more than the prayer.

Out of the total 146.5 verses:

- Agastya said – 6 verses
- *Soota* said – 9.5 verses
- *Śrī Devī* said – 8 verses and the remaining
- 123 verses are told by Lord *Hayagreeva*

Further 300 names are explained one by one prefixed by meaning of preliminary verses, meditation verses and followed by *Phalashrut*i – results of this *Lalitā Triśatī*.

The three hundred names can be chanting as individual names or in the form of verses of couplets. If chant individually, then each name has to be suffixed with '*Namaḥ*' has to be prefixed and suffixed with '*Om*'. However, if the *Triśatī* is chant as a hymn then '*Om*' may be chant at the beginning of each set of 20 names and the rest of the names may be chant like a Hymn, poem or *Stotra* or verse. Many scholars and philosophers have mentioned that chanting of verses and *mantras* without understanding their meanings does not yield any desirable result.

Bhāskararāya in his book "*Varivasya Rahasya*" mentions that: "One who chants a '*mantra*' without understanding its meaning is like one performing '*Yagna*' by throwing dry pieces of wood into a '*Kuṇḍa*', which has no fire. He only feels the pleasure of uttering words. One who chants any *mantras* without understanding the meaning is like a donkey carrying a load of sandal–wood, not being able to feel its aroma but only its weight".

---

[2] The same author has written a book "*Śrī Chakra* – An Esoteric Approach", giving the Mathematical construction to draw *Śrī Chakra* & *Meru* and its parts alongwith the method fo *āvarana* worship.

Hence devotees are requested to understand and comprehend of the meanings of the *mantras* while chanting so that they get the full benefit of chanting.

*****

पूर्व भागः *Pūrva Bhāgaḥ* (Beginning Part)

The *poorva bhāga* or prologues part of *Lalitā Sahasranāma* is in the form of dialogue between sage Agastya and Lord Hayagreeva. But here it is as if narrated by Soota. In the middle Sage Agastya, Lord Hayagreeva and *Śrī Devī* herself utter some words.

अगस्त्य उवाच – *Agastya Uvāca* – Sage Agastya said;

हयग्रीव दया सिन्धो भगवन् शिष्य वत्सल । त्वत्तः श्रुतमशेषेण श्रोतव्यं यद्यदस्तितत् ॥ १

Hayagrīva Dayā Sindho Bhagavan Śişya Vatsala I
Tvattaḥ Śrutamaśeşena Śrotavyam Yadyadastitat II 1

Hayagreeva, who is the ocean of love and compassion, was always fond of his devotees. He always gave his devotees whatever they required. I have learnt whatever was supposed to learn from him.

रहस्य नाम साहस्रमपि त्वत्तः श्रुतं मय । इतः परं मे नास्त्येव श्रोतव्यमिति निश्चयः ॥ २

Rahasya Nāma Sāhasramapi Tvattaḥ Śrutam Maya I
Itaḥ Param Me Nāstyeva Śrotavyamiti Niścayaḥ II 2

As I have learnt the holy, sacred names of *Śrī Lalitāmbikā* from him (Lord Hayagreeva) I have nothing more to learn from him.

तथापि मम चित्तस्य पर्याप्तिर्नैव जायते । कात्स्नर्यार्थः प्राप्त इत्येव शोचयिष्याम्यहं प्रभो ॥ ३

Tathāpi Mama Cittasya Paryāptirnaiva Jāyate I
Kātsnaryārthaḥ Prāpta Ityeva Shocayishyāmyaham Prabho II 3

But my inner feeling says that I have something more to learn from you.

किमिदं कारणं ब्रूहि ज्ञातव्यांशोऽस्ति वा पुनः । अस्ति चेन्मम तद्ब्रूहि ब्रूहित्यक्त्वा प्रणमय तम् ॥ ४

Kimidam Kāranam Brūhi NjātavyāmshoSSti Vā Punaḥ |
Asti Cenmama Tadbrūhi Brūhityktvā Praṇamaya Tam II 4

What is the reason? I am prepared to receive whatever you say and learn.

सूत उवाच – *Sūta Uvāca* – Sage Soota said;

समाललंबे तत्पाद युगळं घटोद्भव: । गयाननो भीतभीत: किमिदं किमिदं त्विति ॥ ५

Samālalambe Tatpāda Yugalam Ghaţodbhavaḥ |
Gayānano Bhītabhītaḥ Kimidam Kimidam Tviti || 5

Sage Agastya held the feet of his *Guru*, Lord Hayagreeva with reverence and the Lord was startled and was gripped with fear.

मुञ्चमुञ्चेति तं चोक्त्वा चिन्ताक्रान्तो बभूव स: । चिरं विचार्य निश्चिन्वन् वक्तव्यं न मयेत्यसौ ॥ ६

Muncamunceti Tam Coktvā Cintākrānto Babhūva Saḥ |
Ciram Vicārya Niścinvan Vaktavyam Na Mayetyasou II 6

Lord Hayagreeva tried to get away from the grip of Agastya and was filled with agony. He thought for a long time and felt that there was nothing more to tell him.

तूष्णीं स्थित: स्मरन्नाज्ञां ललिताम्बाकृतां पुरा। प्रणम्य विप्रं समुनिस्तत्पादावत्यजन्स्थित: ॥ ७

Tūśnīm Sthitaḥ Smrannānjām Lalitāmbākrutām Purā |
Praṇamya Vipram Samunistatpādāvatyajansthitaḥ II 7

Lord Hayagreeva remained silent recalling the order given to him by *Śrī Lalitāmbik*ā in the past. Sage Agastya was still holding the feet of Hayagreeva tightly.

वर्षत्रयावधि तथा गुरुशिष्यौ तथा स्थितौ । तच्छृण्वन्तश्च पश्यंत: सर्वे लोका: सुविस्मिता: ॥ ८

Varşatrayāvadhi Tathā Guruśişyou Tathā Sthitou |
Tacchrumvantaśca Paśyantaḥ Sarve Lokāḥ Suvismitāḥ II 8

Sage Agastya sincerely worshipped Lord Hayagreeva for three years. Seeing the *guru* and the disciple the three worlds was astonished.

तत्र श्री ललितादेवी कामेश्वरसमन्विता । प्रदुर्भूय हयग्रीवं रहस्येवमचोदयत् ॥ ९

Tatra Śrī Lalitā Devī Kāmeśvara Samanvitā |
Pradurbhūrya Hayagrīvam Rahasyevamacodayat II 9

*Śrī Lalitāmbik*ā and Lord *Kāmeśvara* appeared in front of Lord Hayagreeva and told him the following verses in secrecy.

श्रीदेवी उवाच – *Śrī Devī Uvāca – Śrī Devī* said

आश्वाननावतो: प्रीति: शास्त्रविश्वासिने त्वयि। राज्यं देयं शिरो देयं न देया शोडशाक्षरी ॥ १०

Āśvānanāvatoḥ Prītiḥ Śāstraviśvāsine Tvayi |
Rājyam Deyam Śiro Deyam Na Deyā Śoḍashāksharī II 10

Lord Hayagreeva (Horse faced) was a strong believer in *shastras*, they had confidence in him and he was dearer to them. They added that a head can be severed and a kingdom can be given but not the *Shoḍashākṣarī manta*.

स्वमातृज्तरवद्भोप्या विद्यैषत्यागमा जगु:। ततोऽतिगोपनिया मे सर्वपूर्तिकरी स्तुति: ॥ ११

Svamātrujtaravadbhopyā Vidyaiṣatyāgamā Jaguḥ |
Tato(A)Tigopaniyā Me Sarvapūrtikarī Stutiḥ II 11

Scriptures say that the clandestine relationship of a mother should be kept confidential; *Śoḍasī mantra* should be kept in more secrecy than that. This vidyā fulfills all our desires, hence it is called *Sarvapūrtikarī*. In this hymn itself this *Triśatī* Stotra, has been mentioned as *Sarvapūrtikarī* Stotra in multiple places.

मया कामेश्वरेणापि कृता साङ्गोपिता भृशम। मदाज्ञया वचोदेव्यश्चक्रुर्नामसहस्रकम् ॥ १२

Mayā Kāmeśvarenāpi Krutā Sāngopitā Bhruśama |
Madānjayā Vacodevyaścakrarurnāmasahasrakam II 12

The *Triśatī* uttered by us is very secretive and we ordained the *Vāgdevees* to do the *Sahasranāma*.

आवाभ्यां कथिता मुख्या सर्वपूर्तिकरी स्तुति:। सर्वक्रिताणां वैकल्यपूर्तिर्यज्जपतो भवेत् ॥ १३

Āvābhyām Kathitā Mukhyā Sarvapūrtikarī Stutiḥ |
Sarvakritānām Vaikalyapūrtiryajjapato Bhavet II 13

This *Triśatī* articulated by us is very important. Whoever does this *Japa* gets whatever he needs and all his desires are fulfilled. He will achieve success in all his endeavours and will overcome all his obstacles.

सर्व पूर्तिकरं तस्मादिदं नाम कृतं मया। तद्ब्रूहि त्वमहस्त्याय पात्रमेव न संशय: ॥ १४

Sarva Pūrtikaram Tasmādidam Nāma Krutam Mayā |
Tadbrūhi Tvamahastyāya Pātrameva Na Samshayaḥ II 14

The name *Sarvapoortikaree* is given by us. Hence, please give this to Agastya, who richly deserves to get this *mantra*. Do not ever doubt this.

पत्नयस्य लोपामुद्राख्या मामुपास्तेऽतिभक्तितः । अयञ्च नितरां भक्तस्तस्मादस्य वदस्व तत् ॥ १५

Patnayasya Lopāmudrākhyā MāmupāsteSTibhaktitaḥ |

Ayanjca Nitarām Bhaktastasmādasya Vadasva Tat II 15

Lopāmudra, wife of Agastya worships me. Agastya is also my ardent devotee. Hence, please give *Triśatī* to Agastya.

अमुञ्चमानस्त्वद्पादौ वर्षत्रयमसौ स्थितः । एतज्ञातुमतो भक्त्या हितमेव निदर्शनम् ॥ १६

Amunjcamānastvadpādou Varşatrayamasou Sthitaḥ **|**
Etanjātumato Bhaktyā Hitameva Nidarśanam **II 16**

To get this *Upadesa* Agastya was holding your feet for three years. is he not praise worthy?

चित्तपर्याप्तिरेतस्य नान्यथा संभविष्यती। सर्वपूर्तिकरं तस्मादनुज्ञातो मया वद ॥ १७

Cittaparyāptiretasya Nānyathā Sambhavişyatī |
Sarvapūrtikaram Tasmādanunjāto Mayā Vada II 17
Any other thing will not satisfy him except this sacred *Triśatī*. Hence, I ordain you to initiate this holy *mantra* to Agastya.

सूत उवाच – *Sūta Uvāca* – Soota said;

इत्युक्त्वान्तरधदाम्बा कामेश्वरसान्विता । अथोत्थाप्य हयग्रीवः पाणिभ्यां कुम्भसम्भवम् ॥ १८
संस्थाप्य निकटेवाच उवाच भृश विस्मितः ।

Ityuktvāntaradhadāmbā Kāmeśvarasānvitā |
Athotthāpya Hayagrīvaḥ Pānibhyām Kumbhasambhavam II 18
Samsthāpya Nikatevāca Uvāca Bhruśa Vismitaḥ |

Disclosing this, the divine couple disappeared, leaving Hayagreeva in a trance. Then, Lord Hayagreeva carried sage Agastya with both his hands and made him sit next to him. in great astonishment he told him these following words.

हयग्रीव उवाच – *Śrī Hayagrīva Uvāca* – *Śrī Hayagreeva* said;

कृतार्थोऽसि क्रुताथोऽसि क्रुताथोऽसि घटोद्भव ॥ १९ त्वत्समो ललिताभक्तो नास्ति नास्ति जगत्त्रये ।

KrutārthoSSi KrutāthoSSi KrutāthoSSi Ghaţodbhava II 19
Tvatsamo Lalitābhakto Nāsti Nāsti Jagattraye |

Kumbhamunee! You have completed what you were supposed to do. There is nothing else left in this world for you to do. There is no other *Lalitā* devotee equivalent to you in these three worlds.

Note; There are several stories about *Agastya* in our *purāṇas*. The word *Agastya* means, one who made the mountain stay stable. One story relates to *Śrī Agastya* stabilising the *Vindhyā* Mountain, which was going on growing in height. Moreover, it has been stated that *Mitrā* and *Varuṇā*, the two *Vedic* gods were so bewitched by the beauty of the heavenly damsel *Oorvashi* that their semen spilled and a part of it fell in a pot (*kumbha*) and *Agastya* born out of it. Hence, he is variously called as *Kumbhajanma, Ghaḍodbhava, Kumbhayoni, Kalasodbhava*, etc. His height was only that of a thumb, but there was none equal to him in knowledge and power of penance.

एनागस्त्य स्वयं देवी तववक्तव्यमन्वशात् ॥ २०
सच्छिष्येन त्वया चाहं दृष्ट्वानस्मि तां शिवाम् । यतन्ते दर्शनार्थाय ब्रह्मविष्णवीशपूर्वका: ॥ २१

Enāgastya Svayam Devī Tavavaktavyamanvaśāt II 20
Sacchişyena Tvayā Cāham Druştvānasmi Tām Śivām |
Yatante Darśanārthāya Brahmavişnvīśapūrvakāḥ II 21

I had been ordained by *Śrī Devī* to initiate you and hence I had the blessed *darshan* of the divine couple. It was because of the gifted one like you, which even *Brahma, Vişŋu* and *Eesha* have to wait in aspiration.

अत: परं ते वक्ष्यामि सर्वपूर्तिकरं स्थवम् । यस्य स्मरण मात्रेण पर्याप्तिस्ते भवेद्ध्रुदि ॥ २२

Ataḥ Param Te Vakşyāmi Sarvapūrtikaram Sthavam |
Yasya Smaraṇa Mātrena Paryāptiste Bhaveddhrudi II 22

This Stotram, which gives you immense satisfaction and which will fill your void will be initiated to you. When this *Stotram* is recited with single–minded devotion you can see the goddess instantly and implicitly.

रहस्यनाम साह्यस्रादपि गृह्यतमं मुने। आवस्यकं ततोऽप्येतल्ललितां समुपासितुम् ॥ २३

Rahasyanāma Sāhyasrādapi Gruhyatamam Mune |

Āvasyakam TatoऽPyetallalitām Samupāsitum ll 23

This hymn is more secretive than the *Sahasranāma* and is more important to the devotees of *Lalitā*

तदहं संप्रवक्ष्यामि ललिताम्बानुशासनात् । श्रीमत्पञ्चदशाक्षर्या: कादिवर्णान्क्रामन् मुने ॥ २४
पृथग्विंशति नामानि कथितानि घटोद्भव । आहत्य नाम्नां त्रिशती सर्वसंपूर्तिकारणी ॥ २५

Tadaham Sampravakşyāmi Lalitāmbānuśāsanāt |
Śrīmatpanjcadashākşaryāḥ Kādivarnānkrāman Mune ll 24

Pruthagvimśati Nāmāni Kathitāni Ghaţodbhava |
Āhatya Nāmnām Triśatī Sarvasampūrtikāraŋī ll 25

Goddess *Lalitāmbik*ā has ordained me to initiate you this *mantra*. The devotee is very lucky when he is initiated to the hymn containing three hundred names, which are very secretive. It should be kept secretive in high esteem to get the maximum benefits. According to the *kādi vidyā* tradition there are fifteen syllables starting from the letter *'Ka'*. Twenty names start with each of the syllables. *Sarvapūrtikarī Stotram* has three hundred names. Oh, *Kumbhamunee*! all the three hundred names fulfill the desires of the devotees.

रहस्यादिरहस्यैषा गोपनीया प्रयत्नत: । तां श्रृणुष्व महाभाग सावधानेन चेतसा ॥ २६

Rahasyādirahasyaishā Gopanīyā Prayatnataḥ |
Tām Śrunuşva Mahābhāga Sāvadhānena Cetasā ll 26

Oh, Lucky one! This is a kingly secret, secret of secrets. It should be kept secretly and carefully and done with concentrated devotion.

केवलं नामबुद्धिस्ते न कार्य तेषु कुम्भज । मन्त्रात्मकत्वमेतेषां नाम्नां नामात्मतापि च ॥ २७
तस्मादेकाग्रमनसा श्रोतव्यं च त्वया सदा ।

Kevalam Nāmabuddhiste Na Kārya Teşu Kumbhaja |
Mantrātmakatvameteşām Nāmnām Nāmātmatāpi Ca ll 27
Tasmādekāgramanasā Śrotavyam Ca Tvayā Sadā |

Oh Kumbhamunee! Do not think they are just names and be careless. It is *mantra* of *mantras* and name of names. Hence, hear with focused attention and devotion.

सूत उवाच – *Sūta Uvāca* – *Soota* said;

इति उक्त्वा तं हयग्रीव: प्रोचे नामशतत्रयम् ॥ २८

Iti Uktvā Tam Hayagrīvaḥ Proce Nāmaśatatrayam II 28

In this way Lord Hayagreeva started uttering the Sarvapoortikaree Stotram to sage Agastya.

The above clearly, beyond any doubt, conveys the secrecy of *Lalitā Triśatī* hymn. If a devotee like sage Agastya had to struggle so much to learn this hymn, how about lay men like us!

इति श्रीललिता त्रिशती स्तोत्र पूर्व पीठिका सम्पूर्णम् ।

Iti Śrī Lalitā Triśatī Stotra Pūrva Pīṭhikā Sampūrnam

Thus, *Śrī Lalitā Triśatī Stotra Poorva Peeṭhikā* is complete.

*****

Śrī Lalitā Triśatī Japa Vidhānam

(Method of Meditation)

Nyāsa – This is a ritual as part of any *Japa*, in which different aspect of the deity and the *mantras* are invoked in different parts of the body; the head, fingers, etc. Here it is seen the *kavaca*, the armor of the deity being invoked for protection – assignment of the various parts of the body to different deities and corresponding gesticulations.

1. *Oṃ Asya Śrī Lalitā Triśatī Stotra Mahā Mantrasya*
   Vaśinyādi Vāgdevata Rṣayaḥ I
   Anuṣṭup Candaḥ I *Śrī Lalitā Mahā Tripura Sundarī Devatā* I
   Oṃ Im Bījam, *Oṃ Souḥ Śaktiḥ* *Oṃ Klīm Kīlakam* |
   Śrī Lalitā Mahā Tripura Sundarī Prasāda (Mama Caturvidha Purushārta)
   Siddhyartte Triśatī (Jape) Pārāyane Viniyogaḥ |

For this great *Lalitā Triśatī mantra* (a garland of letters) *Vasinee* and other eight *Vāgdevees* are the sages (the sage who first initiated the *mantra*). The meter is *Anuṣṭup* (every verse has 32 syllables). The presiding deity is *Śrī Lalitā Mahā Tripura Sundaree.*

Sages are those who first discovered any *mantra*. Hence before commencing the meditation or recitation of that *mantra*, by way of obeisance to that sage, who gave us that *mantra*, we touch our head with our right hand uttering his name. Next, by way of paying respect to the meter in which the *mantra* is set, we symbolically touch our lips with the right hand – only symbolic because, physical contact with the lips will make the hand impure. Next, we touch our heart to pay respect to the presiding deity of the *mantra*.

Then the three areas of the *mantra* viz., *Bījam, Śak*ti and *Kīlakam*, are indicated. The *mantra*s include, within self, everything seen in this world like the seeds of a banyan tree. Hence the first part is *Bījam* (seed). This seed or the potency contained in the seed is called *Śak*ti (power) – the second part. The third one *Kīlakam* means a nail or peg. It makes the energy of the *mantras* to concentrate in one place instead of unnecessarily getting wasted everywhere. in practice, any *mantra* is split into three – the first one is called *Bījam*, the second *Śakti* and the third – *Kīlakam*. The worshipper has to imagine that these three parts are stabilised in those specific organs of the body by touching the corresponding organs. This is called *Bīja Nyāsam, Śak*ti *Nyāsam* and *Kīlaka Nyāsam*.

2. For *Lalitā Triśatī*, these three – i.e. *Bīja, Śakti* and *Kīlaka* are indicated in

different methods as explained below;

- The 15 letters of *Pancadaśākşarī mantra* are split into three groups viz., *Vāgbhava, Kāmarāja* and *Śakti*. Imagining these three groups as *Bīja, Śakti* and *Kīlaka* is one method. To protect its secrecy the *mantra* cannot be explicitly mentioned here.
- The next method is splitting the *mantra* into 5, 6 and 4 letters and using the same explicitly as *Bīja, Śak*ti and *Kīlaka*.
- Imagining the three letters of *Bālā mantra* as *Bīja, Śakti* and *Kīlaka* individually.
- *Śrī Ādi Shankara* says that the first letters of the three groups' viz., *Ka, Ha* and *Sa* of *Pancadaśākşarī mantra* can be treated as *Bīja, Shakti* and *Kīlaka*.

3. Since this is *nyāsam*, any of the above four methods should be followed as initiated by the teacher. There are different ways in which the organs of the body are to be touched;

- *Bīja* – naval button, *Śakti* – the secret organ and *Kīlakam* – the feet.

Traditionally whatever is taught by the teacher has to be followed.

4. The aim, goal or purpose of the recital follows next. This is called as *Viniyoga Nyāsa* – by touching all the organs with the right hand. It is believed that *Śrī Devī* will accept the recital and will bless the reciter with what is sought for. If any particular wish or requirement is aimed at, that will be fulfilled with her blessings. Thus, *Viniyoga* is done.
5. Some notably worthy points about what was discussed above;

- *Vasinī* and other *Vāgdevīs* are those who did this hymn. Hence, it was mentioned that they are treated as the sages of this *Triśatī* and they are worshipped by touching the head. This is a common rule for chanting of any *mantra*. The concerned sage of the relevant *mantra* has to be thought of. In addition, there is a special reason in the case of this *Triśatī. Śrī Ādi Śaṇkara,* in his *Soundaryalaharī* (17th verse) mentions that whenever *Śrī Lalitā* is thought of, it should be alongwith *Vasinī* and other *Vāgdevīs*;

  Savithrībhirvācām Caśimaṇişilābhangarucibhiḥ
  Vaśinyādhyābhistvām Saha Janani Samchintayati Yaḥ I
- These eight *Vāgdevīs* are worshipped in the eighth hall of *Śrīchakra* called *Sarvarokahara Chakra*; their names are – *Vasinī, Kāmeshvarī, Mohinī, Vimalā, Aruṇā, Jayinī, Sarveshvarī* and *Koulinī.*
- These eight *Devīs* are being worshipped in one other method also. To worship in the four places alongwith *Bhuvaneshwarī*, the mother of the world – the

first four in the triangle and the *Bindu* and the second four in the eight corners, internal ten corners and the external ten corners.

- It was earlier mentioned that the meter of this hymn has to be worshipped as *Anuşţup*. According to *mantra sāstra*, in this *Triśatī*, each of the verses contains 32 letters – i.e. each quarter verse has 8 letters and this meter is called *Anuşţup*. If the entire *Triśatī* is considered, it can be treated as *Mālāmantra*.

Karaşaḍanganyāsās (six Nyāsās in hands)

6. The *karanyāsam* (*nyāsā* of hands) is being done, to sanctify the hands and the fingers, which do many pure and impure actions and hence are not clean. As mentioned earlier the *mantra* to be chant has to be split into six or three parts. With that respectively, the thumbs, fore–fingers, middle–fingers, ring–fingers, little–fingers and the palm and its back are to be cleaned by touching them with each part of six parts or twice the three parts of the *mantra*. This is called *karanyāsam*.

Nyāsās of Six organs

7. Like *karanyāsā* the *mantra* has to be split into six or three parts (as used for *karanyāsa* above). The organs where the *nyāsā* has to be done are heart, head, the hair knot at the back of the head, *kavacha* (shield), eyes and *astra*. The below table details these;

The organ to be touched	The offering *mantra*	The hand to be used	Finger(s) to be used
Heart	*Hrudayāya Namaḥ*	Right	Ring, middle and fore-fingers
Head	*Sirase Svāhā*	Right	Middle and ring fingers
The hair knot at the back of the head or its place, if it is not there.	*Shikāyai Vaśat*	Right	Thumb
Shoulders – both right and left	*Kavacāya–Hum*	Both the hands at a time	All the five fingers

The organ to be touched	The offering *mantra*	The hand to be used	Finger(s) to be used
Two eyes and the middle of the eye brows	*Netratrayāya Voushat*	Right	Ring, middle and fore-fingers (at a time to be touched)
Left Palm	*Astrāyaphaṭ*	Right	Middle and fore-fingers
Around the head from right to left	*Bhūḥ Bhuvaḥ Suvaḥ*	Right	By knuckling middle and fore-fingers.

8. The goal of these *nyāsās*; If this *nyāsā* is done in a concentrated manner before start of the chanting, it is definite that the body of the worshipper himself becomes the form of energy.

   - **Heart** – the place where the presiding deity has to be focused. Hence this place has to be sanctified and bowed.
   - **Head** – the important place of the body where the intellect originates.
   - ***Śikā*** – when the *kundalini* energy traverses to and fro *Moolādhāra* till *Sahasrārā*, it dwells in this place.
   - ***Kavacha*** – a shield to keep off the evil energies without the affecting the worshiper.
   - **Eyes** – to purify the eyes that have to identify the deity. (It is assumed that all of us have three eyes – the third one being hidden between the eye–brows).
   - ***Astrāyaphaṭ*** – Like *Kavacha,* to keep off the evil energies around the head – the *Vyāhruti mantras - Bhūḥ Bhuvaḥ Suvaḥ* is used to bind all the directions.

Meditation Verse

9. The aim of meditation is; The universal absolute, which does not have any form has to imagine with a form to be kept in mind to facilitate worshipping frequently. *Vichekshena Kruhyate* – Since the worshipped deity is imagined in the mind with some identification characters it is called as *Vigraham* (Idol).

अतिमधुरचापहस्तामपरिमितमोद सौभाग्याम् । अरुणामतिशय करुणामभिनव कुलसुन्दरीम् वन्दे ॥

Atimadhuracāpahastāmaparimitamoda Soubhāgyām |
Aruṇāmatiśaya Karuṇāmabhinava Kula Sundarīm Vande II

I Bow before **Her**,

- Who is the Colour of red,
- Who is mercy of mercies,
- Who is epitome of beauty, every minute and second
- Who holds the bow made of sugarcane and
- Who has arrows which bring happiness and prosperity.

Indeed, **she** is the embodiment of kindness and happiness with youthful beauty.

It can be noted that in the meditation verses of *Lalitā Sahasranāma Stotra* also **she** has been compared to *Aruṇām Karuṇātarangitākshīm* – (I meditate upon **her**, who is red in colour and who has compassion moving like waves in the eyes).

Athishaya Karuṇām – *Śrī Devī 's* compassion has been mentioned in multiple places in this *Triśatī* also 9th name – *Karuṇāmrutasāgarā* and 151st name – *Kārunyavigrahā*.

Again, in *Lalitā Sahasranāma* 581st name – *Dayāmūrtiḥ* – दयामूर्तिः 992nd name – *Avyājakaruṇāmūrtiḥ* – अव्याजकरुणामूर्तिः may also be referred in this context.

Five offerings – *Pancha Pooja*

10. Thus, the form of *Śrī Devī* has to be strongly imagined in the mind during chanting. Five offerings have to be made to the form imagined in the mind. These offerings are only imaginative in mind. The 64 offerings and/ or 16 offerings are two types of worship to be done directly. The same is abridged into 5 and done as a sample. Everything used during worship is made with one of the basic five elements. indicating the same. *Śrī Devī* herself and the things used in her worship are all related to the five basic elements. While (mentally) doing this worship, the *bījas* of the five basic elements viz., *Lam, Ham, Yam, Ram* and *Vam* are to be prefixed.

- The fragrant sandal is for *Śrī Devī* who is in the form earth *tattva*.
- The flower given by ether is for *Śrī Devī* who is in the form of ether.
- The fragrant smoke is for *Śrī Devī* who is in the form of air.
- The light is for *Śrī Devī* who is in the form of fire.
- The food is for *Śrī Devī* who is in the form of water.

11. To provide inner meanings and the purposes, the method of worship and the *nyāsās* are discussed above. However, this has to be followed as taught by

the teacher.

12. At the end of the chanting the same has to be re–submitted to *Śrī Devī* by keeping her form in mind, after again doing *Karashaḍanga nyāsās*, reading the meditation verses and doing the five *pooja* as above. Since the presiding deity is a lady, the submission has to be done in the left hand. We did the prayers to the directions from right to left at the beginning of the chanting. Now it has to be undone from left to right as direction *vimoham*.
13. When *Archana* is done with the names mentioned here *Namaḥ* (I bow) has to be suffixed and the *Pranava mantra* (*Oṃ*) has to be used both as a prefix and a suffix as well. For instance, the first name has to be sued as *Oṃ Kakārarūpāyai Namaḥ Oṃ*. This is unusual to the *archanas* done to other gods/ goddesses. Since *Lalitā Sahasranāma* and *Triśatī* are not only names of *Śrī Devī*, but they are individual *mantras* pregnant with *tattvas*, to protect the power of the *mantra* not to spill over it is both prefixed and suffixed with *Oṃ*

Let all the readers understand what is *nyāsa* and why is it done and pray *Śrī Devī* imagining her form in the mind. in this *Triśatī* itself *Śrī Devī* has indicated **herself** as an important devotee; in *Sahasranāma* also 647th name – *Lopāmudrārcitā* – लोपामुद्रार्चिता – *Tripurasiddanta* says that there is no difference between the *mantra*, the sage who found the *mantra* and the presiding deity. Accordingly, *Śrī Devī* got this name. It can also be meant as **She** is prayed as *Lopāmudrā* herself.

*****

श्रीः

Śrī Lalitā Triśatī
300 divine names of *Śrī Lalitā*

Śrīmad Vāgbhava Kūṭam – श्रीमद्वाग्भवकूटम्

Ka – क Series

1. *Kakārarūpā* – ककाररूपा

- Prostrations (*Namaskāra*–s) to **her** who is represented by the letter *ka*–क, that Is, who has the *bījākşara* of *ka* in the beginning of the *mantra*. As per *Soundaryalaharī ka* represents *Śiva*, who is the creator – *Kham Brahma* – '*ka*' represents *Brahma*, water, head and happiness. Hence, *Lalitā* is *Brahma* (*Hiranyagarbha*), who is the creator of the Universe. As representing water, *Ka* has the quality of protecting the world by providing the basic need of all life. As 'head', **She** is the repository of nectar as per *Kundal*ini *Yoga*. Since nectar is in *Sahasradala Padma* (1000 petaled Lotus – in this context 1000 means thousands and not exactly 1000), *Ka* also represents Supreme bliss (*Paramānanda*) and implies *Parabrahmam*. *Ka* is the embodiment of *ka–vidyā* or *Brahma vidyā*.

2. *Kalyāṇī* – कल्याणी

- *Kalyāṇee* means happiness of all kinds starting from the happiness in youthfulness till *Brahmānanda*. As per *Taitreeya* and other *Upanishads* **She** is the embodiment of pure bliss. *Devee*, represents – according to *Shrut*i:
  - Who is endowed with all pleasant qualities.
  - Who is the personification of all arts – 64 *Kalās*. or *Chandrakala*.
- *Śrī Ādi Śaṇkara*'s, commentary of this name is; auspiciousness is happiness. This happiness in worldly activities, as per *Veda* it is health and youth – that is, happiness enjoyed by this body right from general human till four–faced *Brahma*. These are all atom sized drops from the complete bliss. *Śrī Devī* is the complete bliss. As per *Veda* saying – *Vignānamānandam Brahma* – She is the complete bliss in the form of *Brahmam*, without any blemish.
- *Kalyā* – good words, *ana* – to utter. *Kalyām* + *Ana*ti = one who always utters good words.
- According to the *Padma Purāṇā* – in the Malaya Mountain, **she** is worshipped

as *Kalyāṇee*.

- in *Lalitā Sahasranāma* also the name *Kalyāṇee* – कल्याणी (324th) appears, for which *Śrī* Bhāskararāya has given commentary as:
  - One who is in an auspicious form.
  - *Śrī Devī* is the complete auspicious.

3. *Kalyāṇa Guṇaśālinī* – कल्याण गुणशालिनी

- As mentioned in the previous name *Kalyāna* represents happiness and hence, involves complete bliss such as अमोघकाम, सत्यसंकल्प – unparalleled bliss (pure happiness). *Śrī Devī* has all these qualities.
- This will not imply that attributes are given to essentially attribute-less (निर्गुण) *Brahmam*. This relationship between qualified and unqualified of *Brahmam* can only be learnt by practice of meditation – under the guidance of an appropriate teacher.

4. *Kalyāṇa Śailanilayā* – कल्याण शैलनिलया

- *Śaila* is derived from *Śīlaḥ*, which means a huge rocky mountain. *Devee* has an abode in the solid mountain of bliss or whose abode is *Mahā Meru*, which is *Kalyāna Shaila*
- in *Lalitā Sahasranāma* also we read the 55th name as *Sumeru Madhya Śrungasthā* – सुमेरुमध्यश्रृङ्गस्था– the commentary goes as:
  - One who dwells in the central peak of mount *Meru*.
  - *Sumeru* is a golden mountain, which supports the Earth as its base. There are three peaks located triangularly in the center of the mountain and there is another fourth and higher peak at the center of the triangle. The *Śrīnagaram* where *Śrī Devī* dwells is in this fourth peak. These details are beautifully described in *Lalitāstavarāja* written by sage *Durvāsa*.

5. *Kamanīyā* – कमनीया

- *Śrī Devī* is very desirable because **She** is the embodiment of bliss, or *Śrī Devī* is one who grants everything which is desirable for which a devotee prays and hence **She** is desired and worshipped with devotion. For the knowledgeable (*gyānees*) **she** becomes evident as the most beautiful and is hence desirable. Hence this name is applicable to both those who worship her in the form with *Bhak*ti and for those who meditate internally with *gyāna*, those people following *Kādi* or *Hādi Vidyā*. *Lopāmudrā*, wife of sage Agastya is the founder of *Hādi Vidyā*.

6. *Kalāvatī* – कलावती

- *Śrī Devī* is the personification of the 64 *Kalās* (arts). **She** becomes evident to the devotees by the various parts of her body from head to foot. All parts of **her** body from head to foot are the 64 *Kalās*.
- *Kalā* also means *Tantra*. It has been mentioned in *Soundaryalaharī* (verse 31) that there are 64 *Tantras*. **She** has all these as **Her** form.
- in *Lalitā Sahasranāma* also **she** is mentioned as (236th) *Catuṣṣaṣṭi Kalāmayī* – चतुष्षष्टिकलामयी, for which *Śrī* Bhāskararāya has commented;
  - One who embodies the sixty-four forms of arts. **She** has all the arts in **Her** form.
  - The list of 64 arts;

1. The knowledge of the scripts of eighteen languages – Samskruta, Prākrut, Udeechi, Mahārashtree, Magatee, Mishramāgatee, Chakāpeeri, Avanti, Drāvedee, Otriyā, Pāchādyā, Prāchyā, Bāhveekā, Rantikā, Dākshinādyā, Paichachee, Āvantee and Chourasenee.
2. Writing these scripts.
3. The power of writing and reading these languages quickly.
4. Drawing
5. Knowledge of different languages
6. Composing verses in them
7. The art of repeating what is heard.
8. Gambling
9. 9 to 12 – Knowledge of the four *Vedas – Rig, Yajur, Sāma* and *Atharvana*
13. 13 to 16 – Knowledge of the four auxiliary *Vedas – Gāndharvā, Āyur Veda, Danur Veda* and *Artha Sāstra*.
17. 17 to 22 – Knowledge of six *sāstrās – Nyāsa, Vaiseshikā, Sānkhyā, Yoga, Meemamsā* and *Vedanta*.
23. 23 to 28 – Knowledge of six *Vedangas – Shikshā, Vyākaranā, Chandas, Nruktā, Jyothishā* and *Kalpa*.
29. Knowledge of *Tantra Purāṇā* and *Smrutee*
30. Knowledge of poetry, rhetoric and drama
31. 31 to 36 Knowledge of pacifying, controlling, attracting, enmity, ruining by magical practices and killing
37. 37 to 43 The art of opposing the effects of motion, water, sight, fire, weapons, speech and semen
44. The art of making scriptures
45. 45 to 48 Art of training elephants, horses, chariots and men
49. The knowledge of divination by bodily marks (*sāmudrikā*)

50. Art of boxing
51. Art of cooking
52. Art of removing venom
53. Art of playing string instruments
54. Art of playing wind instruments like flute
55. Art of playing percussion instruments
56. Art of playing heavy instruments made of bronze.
57. Creating illusion (*indrajāla*)
58. Art of dancing
59. Art of singing
60. The art of alchemy
61. Knowledge of testing gems
62. Thieving
63. Knowledge of the pulse
64. Art of disappearance

7. *Kamalākṣī* – कमलाक्षी

- Whose eyes are like blossomed lotus
- The word can be split in to *kamalāya akshi* – who is apparent to the eye of knowledge of *Śrī* Lakshmee
- Who is the target of meditation (or knowledge) of Lakshmee – here *Akshi* should be understood as being apparent to *Gnāna*
- It could also mean that great amount of wealth becomes attainable by **Her** one look.
- in *Soundaryalaharī* there are many verses describing the beauty and greatness of eyes of *Śrī Devī*. Specifically, these verses may be referred; 52 to 57 – *Gate Karnābhyarnam, Vibhakta Traivarṇyam, Pavitreekartum Naḥ, Nimeshon Meshābhyām, Tavāparne Karne* and *Drushā Dragheeyasyā*

103rd name of this *Triśatī* – *Hariṇekṣṇā* –हरिणेक्ष्णा, may also be referred.

- In *Lalitā Sahasranāma* also there are many a name describing the beauty of **her** eyes for which Bhāskararāya has commented as:
  - 18 – *Vaktralakshmī Parīvāhacalanmīnābhalochanā* – वक्त्रलक्ष्मी परीवाहचलन्मीनाभलोचना – One whose eyes look like fish swimming in the stream of beauty of *Śrī Devī*'s face.

332 – *Vāmanayanā* – वामनयना – One who has beautiful/ graceful eyes.

561 – *Mrugākṣī* – मृगाक्षी – One who is deer eyed. The eyes of the deer's will not be static at one place – It waves all the sides.

601 – *Darāndolitadīrghākṣī* – दरान्दोलितदीर्घाक्षी – One who has wavering wide eyes extending upto her ears.
936 – *Vishālākṣī* – विशालाक्षी – One who has long and large eyes. The eyes leading upto the ears will be beautiful.

8. *Kalmaṣaghnī* – कल्मषघ्नी

- One who destroys the dirt of sins.
- The fire of *jnana* destroys the fruits of all *karmas* – says *Shruti*
- The One who destroys defaults, blemishes and sins
- This name confirms the Lord Krishna's promise: – I will free you from all sins – अहं त्वा सर्वपापेभ्यो मोक्षयिष्यामि मा शुच: ॥

Aham Tvā Sarvapāpebhyo Mokṣayiṣyāmi Mā Śucaḥ ॥

Shrimad Bhagawad Geeta 18–66

- The word also means the one who is the Knowledge Absolute, which according to the Lord Krishna again, is the Fire of Wisdom that burns to ashes all the luggage of *karma* that one carries along:

ज्ञानाग्नि: सर्वकर्माणि बस्मसात्कुरुते तथा ॥

Jnānāgniḥ Sarva Karmāni Bhasmasātkurute Tathā ॥

Shrimad Bhagawad Geeta 4–37

9. *Karuṇāmruta Sāgarā* – करुणामृत सागरा

- **She** is the like the ocean of nectar in the form of liberation originated by compassion. Ocean does not move from its place, but gives life to the entire world by vaporising its water as clouds and raining in all places based on the temperature.
- Similarly, as *Veda* says – *Brahma Veda Brahmaiva Bhavati* and *Brahmavidāpnoti Param* – **She** is in the form of ocean of nectar of liberation.
- in *Shrimad* Bhagawad Geeta (7–22) Lord *Śrī Krishna* voices as – the worshipper obtains his desires ordained by me;

लभते च तत: कामान्मयैव विहितान्हि तान् ॥

Labhadesa Tataḥ Kāmān Mayaiva Vihitān Hitān ॥

Similarly, **she** provides the strength to all corresponding to the results of the adorations and obligatory duties done by each of the officials.

- **She** is the embodiment of *Brahmam* (immortality) as per *Shruti*

- Who gave *Amruta* and granted heaven (immortality) to the sons of *Sāgara* (सागर);
- Who is *Bhāgīrati*, who went to the ocean (सागर) to get the bliss of *Amruta* (immortality).
- **She** has the duty to protect the devotees surrendered to **Her** – that is compassion. in this fashion also **She** is like an ocean.
- 151st name *Kaṭākṣasyandi Karuṇā* – कटाक्षस्यन्दि करुणा and 153rd name *Kāruṇyavigrahā* – कारुण्यविग्रहा may also be referred.
- The famous *Śrī Śrīdara Venkatesar* also called as *Ayāvāl* has written an epic of poems called *Dayā Shatakam* about compassion. This book has been written metamorphosing the compassion of *Śiva* as another *Devee*. It would be apt to consider the 11th verse of this book here;

  Nānyo Madastyagatiko'gatikastava Śivam
  Shambhor Daye'ghapishunā Mayi Shashva Dāste I
  Sarvagnatā Vidadhāti Tava Durlabham Mām
  Sajjasva Mā Janani Bhūrapade Tu Niḥsvā II
- *Śrī Parāsara Battar* also describes in detail about compassion in his book called *Kshamā Shoḍashee*. In the first verse itself, he says – **She** ensures the safety of the world herself, setting aside the independence of *Śiva*.
- *Śrī Vedanta Desikar* also in his book called *Dayā Shatakam* (verse 51–14) mentions about the compassion of *Śrī Venkatācalapathi* as below:

  Atikrupaṇo'pi Janturadhigamya Daye Bhavateem
  Ashidiladharmasetu Padaveem Ruchiramāchirāt I
  Amita Mahormijālamatilangya Bhavāmbu Nidhim
  Bhavati Vrushāchalesha Padapattana Nityadhanee II
  Krupana Janakalpalatikām Krutāparādhasya Nishkriyāmādhyām I
  Vrushgirināthadaye Tvām Vidanti Samsāratāriṇeem Vibudhāḥ II
- in *Lalitā Sahasranāma* also the same meaning is conveyed in the below names for which *Śrī* Bhāskararāya has commented as:
  - *Karuṇārasa Sāgarā* – करुणारस सागरा (326) – One who is the ocean of compassion as water.
  - *Dayāmūrtiḥ* – दयामूर्तिः (581) – One who is the personification of mercy/ compassion.
  - *Avyājakaruṇāmūrtiḥ* – अव्याजकरुणामोर्तिः (992) – *Śrī Devī* is with so much compassion on **her** devotees without any gambling, dispute, deceit, partiality or expectation.

10. *Kadamba Kānanā Vāsā* – कदम्बकानना वासा

- Who resides in the forest with *Kadamba* trees. *Kadamba* here indicates a kind of *Kalpa Vruksha* – a tree which grants all desires;
- Who resides in the middle of numerous and beautiful trees.
- The 60th name of *Lalitā Sahasranāma* is *Kadamba Vana Vāsinī* – कतम्बवनवासिनी – Only since **She** is fond of *Kadamba* trees; a *Kadamba* jungle has been set up outside her *Chintamani Graham* (house). One who lives in *Kadamba* woods.
- Again, in *Lalitā Sahasranāma* we read the 323rd name as *Kadamba-Kusumapriyā* – कदम्ब कुसुमप्रिया, for which *Śrī* Bhāskararāya has commented as: One who is fond of *Kadamba* flowers.
- *Chintāmaṇigraha* is a palace of gems surrounded by a jungle of *Kadamba* trees. *Śrī Devee* dwells in this jungle.
- *Śrīpura* is surrounded by 25 walls made of metals and gems representing 25 concepts (*Tattvas*). The *Kadamba* jungle is located between the gold and silver walls.
- Madurai (a holy city in Tamilnadu) is also known as *Kadamba Vana*. *Śrī Devee* is the presiding deity here with the name *Meenakshi*. This indicates the goddess *Meenakshi*, who is blessing the devotees at Madurai.

11. *Kadamba Kusumapriyā* – कदम्ब कुसुमप्रिया

- This name is in continuation of the previous name.
- Who loves the blossoms of *Kadamba* trees.
- inner–self is a group of Satva quality of five elements. Similarly, *Kalpaka* tree is a common name for five types of trees viz., *Santānam, Harisantānam, Mantāram, Pārijātam* and *Kadambam*. The five parts of inner self is mind, intellect, volition, ego and heart. Mind is the *sattva* part of wind. intellect is the *sattva* part of fire. Similarly, volition – water, ego – earth and heart or combined inner–self *sattva* part of ether. Hence *Kadamba* is mind;
- One who resides in the forest of mind is called *Kadambavana Vāsā* or *Kadambavana Vā*sinee. *Kadamba Kusumā* is the expansion of the mind. Knowledge and expansion are inseparable forms. There is no knowledge without expansion and vice versa. Hence for *Śrī Devee*, who is in the integrated form of knowledge on subjects and *tattvas*, is very much of fond of *Kadamba* flower in the form of expansion of mind.
- The 323rd name of *Lalitā Sahasranāma, Kadamba Kusuma Priyā* – कदम्बकुसुमप्रिया says that **She** is fond of *Kadamba* flowers.

12. *Kandarpa Vidhyā* – कन्दर्प विध्या

- Who is worshipped by *Kāmadeva*, who understood and realised her.
- *Vidhya* is the term applied to the assemblage of letters chanted as *Mantra*.
- *Upanishad* is the term which implies the words of *Vedas*, which help in the understanding of *Brahma Vidhyā*. *Vidhya* = a *Mantra*, the *Vedic* means for attaining or achieving knowledge of *Brahmam*).
- *Śrī Devī* is understood and worshipped by *Kāmadeva*.

13. *Kandarpa Janakāpāṅga Vīkṣaṇā* – कन्दर्प जनकापाङ्ग वीक्षणा

- *Apāṅga* means crippled Kāmadeva or glance from the eye.
- *Śrī Devī 's* side glance (seeing with half–opened eyes) was responsible for the creation of *Kandarpa* or *Manmatha* or Cupid
- The implication is – even ugly, old, decrepit men become young and handsome and strong as Manmatha by just a side glance from *Śrī Devī;*
- Lord *Viṣṇu*, the father of Cupid was bound to perform the duty of protecting the world having been stimulated by the side glance of *Śrī Devī* 's eyes;
- *Śrī Mahalakshmi*, who is the mother of Cupid, was stimulated by the glance of the half–closed eyes of *Śrī Devī;*
- *Śrī Devī* can bestow the stuffs such as fragrance, flowers and such other enjoyable things, which stimulate what *Kāma* stands for (that is lust for enjoyment) by just a side glance;
- *Kandarpa Janaka* is *Śrī* Mahalakshmi or the seat of *Lakshmee* that is the lotus. Hence a look from *Śrī Devī 's* lotus like eyes is able to grant happiness (bliss) and creative activity of the entire world.

14. *Karpūravīṭi Sourabhya Kallolita Kakuptaṭā* –
कर्पूरवीटि सौरभ्य कल्लोलित ककुप्तटा

- *Tāmbūla* – *Veeda* or *Beeda* – betel leaves mixed with ingredients like lime, petal–nut, etc. *Veetikā* is a small pack (folded inside a betel leaf) with proper mixture of aromatic spices such as camphor, cardamom, cloves, musk, saffron, nutmeg, betel nut, lime, etc.
- The fragrance of *Tāmbūla* mixed with camphor, spreads to the borders of the Universe. Hence *Śrī Devī 's* breath spreads fragrant waves to the very borders of the Universe.
- The whole world is drenched with this aroma emanating from *Śrī Devī*'s mouth and *Śrī Devī* is thus *Maharaja Bhogavathi* (one who enjoys the comforts of an empress)

- *Śrī Ādi Śaṇkara*, while interpreting this name specially indicates as *Maharaja Bogavatee*.
- The 26th name of *Lalitā Sahasranāma – Karpūra Vīṭikāmoda Samākarşidigantarā* – कर्पूरवीटिकामोद समकर्षिदिगन्तरा says that **she** attracts the four directions towards **Her** by the pleasant aroma of the betel (*tambala*) emanating from **Her** lotuslike mouth, or one who spreads that aroma in all directions.
- Again the 559th name of *Lalitā Sahasranāma – Tāmbūla Pūritamukhī* – तांबूलपूरितमुखीsays that one whose mouth is full of betel leaves.
- It is told that legendary poets, like *Kālidāsa, Kālameka* and others, got their excellent capacity to write poems by consuming the juice of *Śrī Devee*'s *tāmbūla* (betel leaves).

15. *Kalidoṣaharā* – कलिदोषहरा

- *Śrī Devī* eradicates all the evils inherent in *Kaliyuga* (era of *Kali*) such as atheism; agnosticism; and useless debates and establishes one–ness of all existence with **Herself** (*Advaita*) in the minds of deluded and confused people.
- The weaknesses inherent in *Kaliyuga* are indicated in *Devī Bhāgavata* 12th *Kāṇḍa* and 9th Chapter.
- in this *Triśatī*, especially in the names beginning with *e*–ए, ee–ई and the conjunction 'and–च' is often prefixed to the name; the implication is –
  - *Brahmam* can be addressed without qualities or attributes *Nirguṇa*–निर्गुण) or with qualities or attributes *Saguna*–सगुण.
  - *Brahmam* can be addressed as female or male (त्वं स्त्री त्वं पुमान्– *Tvam Stree Tvam Pumān* – says *shruti*) or in neuter (तत्सत्यं स आत्मा – *Tat Satyam Sa Ātmā*. *Brahmam* can be addressed in the genderless first person (as in *Aham Brahmāsmi* – अहं ब्रह्मास्मि) or some person (*Tat Tvamasi* – तत् त्वमसि).
  - in this context of the *karma Kāṇḍa* areas of *Shrimad Bhagawad Geeta* can be read properly, not by the ordinarily accepted meanings of the words in the verses.

16. *Kaṅjalocanā* – कञ्जलोचना

- *Kaṅja*–कञ्ज means Lotus (*kan*–कं = water, *ja*–ज = born)
- Who has eyes like lotus

- *Kanja*–कंज also indicates Brahma and hence this name suggests that the whole Universe has arisen from water which was created first;
- *Kanja*–कंज = *Brahmāṇḍa* – the whole Universe; by a glance of **Her** eyes, *Śrī Devī created* the whole Universe.
- *Śrī Devī* directed Brahma to create the Universe by a side glance of the eyes.

17. *Kamravigrahā* – कम्रविग्रहा

- *Śrī Devī has* a beautiful (captivating) form adorned by courage, grace and sweetness.

18. *Karmādi Sākṣiṇī* – कर्मादि साक्षिणी

- *Śrī Devī* is a witness to worship performed as per prescribed *Karmas*.
- *Śrī Devī* becomes apparent (*Sākşātkāra* – साक्षात्कार), through different *karmas* such as *Upāsana* – उपासन, *yagna*, *Śravan* – श्रवण – listening to her prayers.

19. *Kārayitrī* – कारयित्री

- Who evokes prescribed *Karma–s (Vedic Karma–s).*

20. *Karmaphalapradā* – कर्मफलप्रदा

- One who bestows boons for performing prescribed *Karma*–s.
- Who grants the fruits of *Karma*–s (*Karma Meemāmsakas* contend that *Karma* is the ultimate objective and the result *phala* – फल is *adrushta* – अदृष्ट that is unseen. This is not acceptable because *Karma* cannot be motivated without the desire for the fruits and *Karma* per–se becomes meaningless. *Śrī Devī* ensures that the prescribed *Karma* bears the desired fruits. The anticipation is the main stimulus for performing *Karma*.
- *Śrī Ādi Śaṇkara* in his commentary explains – corresponding to the actions, the results will be reaped later. The reason for the same is un–seeable or rareness – argues the atheists (followers of *pūrva meemāmsa*). But this is not true. Un–seeable is so micro or atom level matter that it does not have the capacity to provide fruits. The fruit for every action is definite. It has to be accepted one who gives the fruit for the actions should be superior to the doer of the action – as *Veda* says; *Karmādhyakşaḥ* and as Lord Krishna says *Mayaivi Vihitān* (*Śrīmad Bhagavad Geeta* 7–22) – *Śrī Devī* is the one who provides the fruits based on the actions.

- The dispenser of the fruits of actions. The actions themselves are insentient and hence cannot give their fruits. There must be a sentience behind the dispensing act. It is the Absolute that dispenses. But the Absolute is action less. It can only witness. Everything happens in its presence. The original action happens in and because of, its presence. The dispensing of the fruit also by the *Prakru*ti (the Power or Energy of the Absolute) happens in and because of, its presence.
- The 923rd name of *Lalitā Sahasranāma, Dakṣiṇādakīṣiṇārādhyā* – दक्षिणादक्षिणाराध्या says that **she** is fit to be worshiped by the learned (who has capability) and also by the illiterates (who do not have capability) alike. Any person irrespective of the knowledge does any *karma* gets the desired fruit.

E–ए Series

21. *Ekāra Rūpā* – एकार रूपा

- One who has the form of *E* – ए.
- The second letter of *Pancadashee mantra* is in the form of a triangle – **She** is in that form.
- The innermost triangle of *Śrī Chakra* is the *Yoni chakra* in a triangle form. **She** is in that form.
- As per *Soundaryalaharī E*– ए stands for *Shak*ti – embodiment of Power, which is the second letter of *Pancadaśākṣarī Mantra*.
- The 986th name of *Lalitā Sahasranāma, Trikoṇagā* – त्रिकोणगा – One who resides in the *Yoni chakra*, which is in the form of a triangle.

22. *Ekākṣarī* – एकाक्षरी

- The only one (*Eka* – एक), who does not get destroyed (*Akṣara Na Kṣaratīti* – अक्षर न क्षरतीति).
- This implies eternality and omniscience. Such a *Māyā* does not get destroyed until self–realisation resulting in *Moksha* (freedom from the cycle of birth and death);
- Who is represented by one letter – the *Praṇava Oṃ* or *Hrīm*;
- Who has become one with eternal *Śiva* by becoming half of the body of *Eeshwara* in *Ardhanareeshwara*.

23. ***Ekānekākṣarākruti**ḥ* **– एकानेकाक्षराकृतिः**

- **She** shines in both the forms, that of a single syllable (*Ekākshara*) *Praṇava* – *Oṃ* – ॐ or *Hrīm* – ह्रीं and that of multiple syllables (*Anekākshara*) – *ka* – क to *Hrīm* – ह्रीं as in the *Pancadashākharee* or all letters of the alphabet from *a* – अ to *ksha* – क्ष;
- **She** is actually 'One' but, **her** forms can be realised (understood) through many kinds of knowledge (*Akshara*–s) or paths – such as by *Bhak*ti, *Karma* and *Gnāna* or by going through various systems of *'Yoga'* (*Rāja Yoga, Kundal*ini *Yoga*, etc.)
- What does this mean? **She** is both *māyā* (deception, illusion) and *avidyā* (ignorance). The first one is the adjunct of the Lord and it is in **His** control. its symbolism is the single syllable *Oṃ* that represents the absolute transcendental truth. *Avidyā* (ignorance) on the other hand is the adjunct of the individual souls and its multiplicity is as infinite as the number of individual souls. *Avidyā* is individual ignorance that clings to the soul and prevents it from realising its transcendental nature whereas *māyā* is cosmic ignorance, which is in the complete control of the Lord. It is *prakruti* – *Śrī Devī* becomes both.
- One who has countless letters/ syllables as **Her** form.
- *Śrī Chitānanda Nāda* talks about *Śrī Ādi Śaṇkara*'s commentary – **She** is in the form of single letter as well as many lettered. The illusion which is the pure *sattva* form or ignorance is single letter form. The cheap ignorance in the form of *sattva* or ignorance is the limitation of the soul. Since there are many souls, so as their limitations also. Hence the word many has been used. According to *Veda* saying; *Māyā Chāvidyā Cha Svayameva Bhava*ti – *Śrī Devī* is the illusion, which is a limitation of *Eshwara* and also the ignorance, which is the limitation of the souls. Again, *Veda* says; *Māyām Tu Prakrutim* – *Śrī Devī* is in the form of one and reflecting as many or the limitations of *Eshwara* and the souls.
- The 757th name of *Lalitā Sahasranāma* – *Kṣarākṣarātmikā* – क्षराक्षरात्मिका also says – one who resides in the *Yoni chakra*, which is in the form of a triangle.
- *Devi Upanishad* says that **She** is in the form of countless *mantras*; *Mantranām Mātrukā Devee*. *Mantras* are formed with letters and **She** is said as to have the form of countless letters.
- The *Varāha Purāṇa* says, "Though *Śrī Devee* is all–syllabled, yet **She** is called mono–syllabled, **she** is the ruler of the universe, **she** alone is all–syllabled"; *Ekākṣareti Vikhyātā Sarvākṣaramayī Śubhā* I
- All living beings are perishable – they are *Kshara*–क्षर (multiform), *Akhsara*–

अक्षर (syllables) and *Ātma* (soul), **Her** body; i.e. **She** is one–syllabled and multi–syllabled as well.

- *Khsara*–क्षर is applied to all beings and *akshara*–अक्षर to *Kooṭastha* (Lord) – **She** is both – vide *Śrīmad Bhagavad Geeta* (XV–16); *Bhootāni Kooṭasthokshara Uchyate* II This name says that *Śrī Devee* thus has two different types of forms.
- 480th and 481st names of *Viṣṇu Sahasranāma – Ksharam* and *Aksharam* also convey the same meaning.
- The *Viṣṇu Bhagavatam* also says the same message, "There are three forms of *Viṣṇu* called *purushas*, those who know say, the first is the creator of the *Mahat*, the second is the mundane egg, the third is what resides in all beings, by knowing this one is released";

Viṣnostu Trīni Rūpāni Puruṣākhyāni Ye Viduḥ I
Pratamam Mahataḥ Sraṣṭā Dvtīyam Tvandasamsthitam II
Trutīyam Sarvabhūtastham Tāni Gnātvā Vimuchyate II

24. ***Etattaditya Nirdeśyā*** **– एतत्तदित्य निर्देश्या**

- Who cannot be defined (designated) as 'This ' or 'That'.
- Who cannot be seen as an actuality (*Pratyaksha* – प्रत्यक्ष) or virtuality or not apparent (*Apratyaksha* – अप्रत्यक्ष);
- *Śrī Devī* cannot be defined in terms of physical actuality or by any description). For defining any one, it is necessary that the person should possess qualities such as shape, size, action etc. and should have existence in time and space. But *Śrī Devī* is *Nirguṇa* – निर्गुण, (attribute-less) beyond time, space and cause and hence beyond description or recognition (*Aśabdamasparśa Arūpyamavyayam* – अशब्दमस्पर्श अरूप्यमव्ययम्, *Nirguṇam Niṣkalam* – निर्गुणम् निष्कलम्) beyond speech, touch mind and comprehension, without attributes; It is *ashabdam*, not describable by sound sense, *asparsham*, not indictable by the sense of touch, *avyayam* immutable, *nirguṇam* with no attributes, *nishkalam* with no marks or specifications. Then how can it be at all described? The scriptures say it is not that which is described by speech but it is that which makes speech possible; it is not what is seen by the eyes, but it is that which makes the eyes see. Hence how can it be decided whether it is this or that? is it the cause, which is invisible or the effect which is visible? It cannot be exclusively pointed to one of them and say it is only that and not this. It is not just this individual soul, nor is it just that Absolute, without reference to the individual soul. The individual soul has certain qualities like ignorance which do not belong to it absolutely and the Absolute has certain facets like the

capability to create, which is only a temporal phenomenon and not a definitive facet. Hence in this sense it is not possible to say it is this or that exclusively.

- Who cannot be defined on the principle of "action and result (*kāryakārana* – कार्यकारण)".
- **She** cannot be pinpointed as this or that. This is the literal meaning of this name. But its meaning goes deeper. The word '*etat*' meaning 'this' signifies the visible universe, which is perceptible to the senses. The word '*tat'* signifies 'that' and points to that Cosmic Absolute Truth which is transcendent and imminent and further is never perceptible to the senses. This *(Etat* – एतत्) refers to present and that (*tat* – तत्) refers to past. Hence *Śrī Devī* is timeless and eternal (*Pratyaksha* – प्रत्यक्ष – visible), seen by oneself; (*Apratyaksha* – अप्रत्यक्ष) not seen by oneself); *paroksha* – परोक्ष seen by others or evidence from other's experience or expression.
- As per *Sānkhya* philosophy an attribute-less, timeless entity, that is God, cannot and does not exist.
- As per *Vişŋu Bhagavata* philosophy *Vişŋu* is the only existence. The *Upanishadic* philosophy is opposed to both these conclusions and accepts that *Jeeva* – soul is the only reality. That is, 'SELF' is the only reality or *Eeshwara* is the only reality. The term *Devata* is explained as the only truth (*sat* – सत्) and bliss (*Ananda* – आनन्द) in *Chāndogya Upanishad*. Since two entities cannot exist together, the identity of *Jeeva* with *Eeshvara* has to be accepted, as mentioned *Ekamevādviteeyam* –एकमेवाद्वितीयं = one only and not two).
- The 426th name of *Lalitā Sahasranāma* – *Tvam* – त्वम् also says – Thou. Among the 36 *tattvas*, the *Śiva tattva* is called *Parā Samvit*. This is the Supreme Being without any quality or blemish. Hence, the *Śiva Tatva* without any dispositions and the *Shak*ti *Tatva*, the cause of the dispositions on account of creation, are one and the same in the *Parā Samvit*. Hence when *Śrī Devee* is in the form of *Parabrahmam*, **She** is referred to as *Prakāsha Vimarsha Sāmarasya Rūpinī*. *Kāmeshwarī* is in the form of brightness. This form of knowledge is integrated with *Aham* (I–self), *Idam* (this), *Etat* (these) and *Tat* (that).

25. *Ekānanda Cidākrutiḥ* – एकानन्द चिदाकृति:

- Who has the form of the only permanent bliss *Ānanda* and consciousness (*chit* – चित्) as mentioned in *Vedas* – *Vijānamānamdam Brahma* – विज्ञानमानंदं ब्रह्म;

- Who has the united form of *Śiva*, who is the embodiment of supreme bliss and *Eeshvara*, who is the embodiment of consciences *chit* – चित्.

26. *Evamityāgamābodhyā* – एवमित्यागमाबोध्या

- *Śrī Devī* cannot be addressed (described) as 'this' or in any specific manner according to *Āgama* (scriptures) principles – Worship, *Pooja*, sacred–rites, *Arcana*, etc., are all included in the term *Āgama* – आगम.
- It is not possible to address *Brahma* by any kind of worship or *Āgama*. The concept of *Brahma* is represented in the phrase *Satya Gnām Anantam* – सत्यज्ञानमानतम् truth, knowledge and unending or limitless or eternal.
- *Brahmam* or *Śrī Devī* cannot be designated by any material form of description. Hence, it is necessary to address and realise *Śrī Devī* as defined by the statement *Tatvamasi* – तत्वमसि (you are that) – the *Advaitic* concept. (The entire *Triśatī* is *Advaitic* and preaches one–ness of *Śrī Devī* with all existence and is absolute – which should necessarily mean– 'I' (*Aham* – अहं) cannot be separate from *Brahmam* – "I and *Brahmam*" are 'one' and there are no–two entities – *Ekamevādvetīyam* – एकमेवाद्वेतीयं.

27. *Ekabhaktimadarcitā* – एकभक्तिमदर्चिता

- Who is worshipped by those who have attained the capacity for concentrated devotion through internal worship (*Antaryāga* – अन्तर्याग), external worship (*Bahiryāga* – बहिर्याग) and great focused devotion (*Mahāyāga* – महायाग);
- *Śrī Devī* is worshipped by those who have realised one–ness of the 'self' with *'Brahmam'*.
- The functions of all senses depend on the mind. Hence, as one meditates or thinks seriously, so does one speak and perform (*Yanmanasā Dhyāyati Tadvācā Vadati Tat Karmanā Karoti* – यन्मनसा ध्यायति तद्वाचा वदति तत् कर्मणा करोति). Hence, *bhak*ti is a function or character of the mind and if centralised, would result in the proper expression and action. Hence, one with concentration – centralised or focussed *bhak*ti can do the *Arcana* or *Pooja* and such persons can achieve *Śrī Devī*.

28. *Ekāgracitta Nirdhyātā* – एकाग्रचित्त निर्ध्याता

- Who has been achieved by those *yog*is who have contemplated with single–minded devotion;

- Who has been attained by;
  - *Ritambharas* (ऋतं + भरती = a condition of *Samādhi*, in which one achieves the condition of *Brahmatva*)
  - *Pragnalokas*, who perceive through *Gnāna* and
  - *Prashanta Vahitas*, those for whom the qualified universe, i.e. *Sākara Prakruti*, has become unqualified i.e. *Nirākāra* and hence beyond time and space and causation).
- Hence, *Ekāgracitāḥ* – एकाग्रचित्त: are those who are in a state of super consciousness and to whom the creator and the created merge and they realise universality and one–ness of all *(Brahma Veda Brahmaiva Bhavati* – ब्रह्म वेद ब्रह्मैव भवति) = one who understands Brahmam becomes Brahmam. For such persons only *Śrī Devī* becomes the reality (*Sākshātkāra* – साक्षात्कार).

29. *Eṣaṇā Rahitāddhrutā* – एषणा रहिताद्धृता

- *Śrī Devī* becomes the reality only for those who have been released from all desires. (*Eṣaṇā* is desire).
- Desire is of three kinds–
  - Desire for comfort and happiness in this living world (*Vittaishanā* – वित्तैषणा, *Lokaishaŋā* – लोकैषणा) that includes desire for children (पुत्रैषणा), etc.;
  - Desire for happiness in the next world, that is, *Pitruloka* and
  - Desire for the attainment of *Devaloka* (दारैषणा).
- Those who have become free from all such desires are referred to as *Paramahamsas* – who have conquered their minds making it free from all desires and therefore become united with *Paramānanda* – eternally blissful.
- Those who have these desires even go for begging for the fulfilment of these desires. But those who wish for freedom indulge in focussed meditation. They are *sanyāsis*. They achieve result in the form of freedom – *moksha*.

30. *Elāsugamdhi Cikurā* – एलासुगंधि चिकुरा

- One who has the front locks of hair which has the fragrance of cardamom. (Her entire body emits fragrance. The frontal hair has been taken as an example of a part of her body).
- in the meaning for the 13th name of *Lalitā Sahasranāma* – *Champakāśoka Punnāga Sougandhikalasatkachā* – चंपकाशोक पुन्नाग सौगन्धिकलसत्कचा, the word *Sougandhi* denotes one flower or good fragrance of all the flowers. Based on this meaning a solution for the question in *Tiruvilayadal Purāṇa* can be found – whether the hair of the ladies has fragrance on its own or on account of the

flowers adoring the hair. in the dispute, in this regard, between *Śrī Parameshvara* and a devotee called *Nakkeera, Nakkeera* was burnt. He boldly argued with *Parameshvara* that even when you show your third eye, the fault is fault only and hence he was burnt. This story was mentioned by *Tetiyoor Brahma Śrī Sāstrigal* in his meaning for *Soundaryalaharī*. The below verse from *Hālāsya Māhātmya* says that on account of this debate, he had to take one more birth before attaining salvation;

Ambāparadhato Muktim Nakkeero Naiva Gachchati I
Ambāparadhato Bhūyaḥ Muktimāpa Dhvijottamaḥ II

- in the 43rd verse of *Soundaryalaharī, Dhunotu Dhvāntam, Śrī Ādi Śaṇkara* conveys through the word *Sahajam* that the fragrance of the hair of *Śrī Devī* is very natural. This clearly indicates that *Śrī Ādi Śaṇkara* is the incarnation of *Śrī Parameshwara*.
- in the 13th name of *Śrī Lalitā Sahasranāma, Śrī* Bhāskararāya says that the fragrance is due to the flowered adoring *Śrī Devī*'s hair. This indicates that he is the incarnation of *Nakkeera*.

31. *Enaḥ Kūṭa Vināśinī* – एन: कूट विनाशिनी

- Who destroys the collection of sins.
- Sins are of three kinds – *Prārabdha* (sins from past births that have led to the current birth), *Sanchita* (sins from past births which are set to fructify in future births) and *Āgāmi* (the sins performed after one becomes knowledgeable).
- **She** destroys all types of sins. If one thinks that these sins can be destroyed by sub–merging in these worldly enjoyments, it can never happen. But with the blessings of *Śrī Devī*, who is in the form of pure self *Brahmam* integrated with the philosophical knowledge, they are completely ruined.
- in *Veda* (*Chāndokya Upanishad* IV–24–3) it is mentioned as:
  Yateshikā Toolamagnou Pradooyataiva Mevāsya Papmanaḥ Pradooyante – Like the point of a reed in the fire, all the sins are burnt up.
- *Vashiṣṭa* Smruti says:

Vidyā Tapobhyām Samyaktam Brāhmanam Japa Naityakam I
*Sadā*pi *Pāpa Karmānameno Na Pradhiyujyate* II
Jāpinām Hominām Chaiva Dhyāyinām Teerthavāsinām I
Na Samvasanti Pāpāni Ye Cha Snātāḥ Shirovrataiḥ II

If a person is always devoted to learning, penance and continually repeating *mantras*, even if he is always committing sinful actions, he is not afflicted thereby. Sin never touches those who repeat the *mantras* or offer oblations, or meditate, or make pilgrimages, or who perform *Shirovrata* (the rite of carrying the fire on the head).

- in the *Padma Purāṇa*, in its *Pushkara Kāṇḍa*, it has been mentioned that – The mass of sins though as great as mount *Meru* is instantly destroyed by worshipping *Kātyāyanee*. He, who is devoted to Goddess *Durgā*, is not stained even by committing heinous crimes, in the manner as the lotus leaf is not affected by water;

  Meru Parvata Matropi Rashiḥ Pāpasya Karmaṇaḥ I
  Kātyāyaneem Samāsādya Nashyati Kshaṇamātrataḥ II
  Durgārchanaroto Nityam Mahāpātaka Sambhavaiḥ I
  Doshair Na Lipyate Veera Padmapatramivāmbhasā II

- in *Saptaśatī* (12th chapter) it is said as; *Srutam Harati Pāpāni* – even if anyone just hears the *Saptaśatī* read by others, the sins are destroyed.
- in *Devee Bhagavatam* also same effect is spoken:

  Chitvā Bhitvā Ca Bhootāni Hatvā Sarvamidam Jagat I
  Praṇamya Shirasā Deveem Na Sa Pāpair Vilipyate II
  Sarvāvastāgato Vāpi Yuktovā Sarvapatakaiḥ I
  Durgām Drushitvā Naraḥ Pootaḥ Prayāti Paramam Padam II

- Again, in *Brahmaṇḍa Purāṇā*;

  Varṇāsrama Viheenānām Papishtānām Nrunāmapi I
  Yadroopa Dhyāna Matrena Dushkrutam Sukrutāyate II

  The sinful actions of those who are devoid of *Varṇa* and *Ashrama* and the wretched also, by mere meditation on *Devee*, become virtuous.

- This has been evidenced by the Lord Krishna also:
  Aham Tva Sarvapāpebhyo Mokshayishyāmi
  अहं सर्वपापेभ्यो मोक्षयिष्यामि *Śrīmad Bhagavad Geetā* (18–66)
- 112th name – *Hatyādi Pāpaśamanī* – हत्यादि पापशमनी may also be referred.
- For the following names of *Śrī Lalitā Sahasranāma*, *Śrī* Bhāskararāya says;
  - 167 – *Pāpanāśinī* – पापनाशिनी – One who destroys the sins of devotees.
  - 555 – *Kalikalmaṣanāśinīe* – कलिकल्मषनाशिनी – One who is destroyer of sin/ transgression of *Kali*.
  - 743 – *Pāpāraṇyadavānalā* – पापारण्यदवानला – One who is like a forest fire that burns down and destroys all the sins.
  - 860 – *Akāntā* – अकान्ता – One who removes sins. *Aka* – sin or sorrow. **She** destroys them. Hence *Akānta*.

32. *Ekabhogā* – एकभोगा

- For whom there is only one object of enjoyment

- Who is the object of enjoyment, of only one (that of *Kāmeshvara*).

33. *Ekarasā* – एकरसा

- Who has only one *Rasa* – feeling, sense of pleasure;
- For whom all *Rasas* are the same (*samarasa* – समरस)
- Who has only *Madhura Rasa* (sweetness) towards all
- Who has only *Srungāra Rasa*, which is the most pleasurable and Important and the first among the nine *Rasas*.

34. *Ekaiśvarya Pradāyinee* – एकैश्वर्य प्रदायिनी

- One who grants immeasurable wealth or the wealth of all kinds
- Who grants the wealth of knowledge that there is only one *Eeshvara*.
- Who bestows the fortune of knowing that *Eeshvara* is the only one basic Truth
- Who gives the knowledge of being one with *Eeshvara*
- Who grants the boon of becoming one with *Eshvara*, *Ekamevādviteeyam* – एकमेवाद्वितीयम् – one and not a second; or one who has no second.
- Also, *Tat Tvamasi* – तत् त्वमसि = 'you are that' – same as, 'you and that' are same.
- Who grants 'one–ness' with *Eeshvara*

35. *Ekātapatra Sāmrājyapradā* – एकातपत्र साम्राज्यप्रदा

- Who grants the boon of feeling like the monarch over all things in the world
- Who grants the boon of complete ruler ship over everything or *Ekātapatra* – एकातपत्र, which means the destruction of *Ajāna* – अज्ञान, (ignorance), which is the basic cause of all unhappiness in the world.
- This implies *Śrī Devī* grants *Ātmajāna* – आत्मज्ञान, which destroys all miseries in this *Samsāra*.

36. *Ekānta Pūjitā* – एकान्त पूजिता

- One who is worshipped in solitude with single mindedness
- Who reveals **Herself** as the only central reality when meditated internally
- All internal meditations ultimately end in the one *Brahmam* that is – *Śrī Devī* (This is also implied in the statement – all *pranāms* lead to the same Lord

Keshava – Sarvadeva Namaskāraḥ Śrīkeśavam Prati Gachchati – सर्वदेव नमस्कार: श्रीकेशवं प्रति गच्छति).

37. *Edhamānaprabhā* – एधमानप्रभा

- One who is increasingly illuminated or who is ever increasing in brightness – brilliance.
- *Kaṭopanishad* (II–2–15) says, The Sun, the Moon and the stars do not shine by themselves; for **She** illuminates the mind that illuminates all of these:

Na Tatra Sooryo Bhāti Na Chandra Tārakam Nema
Vidyuto Bhānti Kutoyamagniḥ Tameva Bhāntamanubhāti
Sarvam Tasya Bhāsa Sarvamidam Vibhāti

38. *Ejadanejaj Jagadīśvarī* – एजदनेजज्जगदीश्वरी

- Who lords over many universes, which **She** stirs and moves
- Who stirs or moves all kinds of living and non–living objects in the universe.

39. *Ekavīrādi Samsevyā* – एकवीरादि संसेव्या

- *Ekaveeras* are those who have uncommon power by which they have obtained all the *Purushārthas* – पुरुषार्थ. *Śrī Devī* is served by such *Ekaveeras*.
- *Ekaveeras* refers to the group of *Shak*ti *Devatas* such as *Renuka*, *Shyāmala* etc. *Śrī Devī* is served by such *Ekaveeras* and others.
- These *Shakti Devis* are established in their respective *Shakti Peeṭas* (in 50 *Shakti Peeṭas*). They represent *Śrī Devī* in different forms. Hence, *Śrī Devī* is also referred to as *Panchāśat Pīṭharūpiṇī* – पञ्चाशत्पिठरूपिणी – 833rd name in *Lalitā Sahasranāma* – One who is the form of fifty *peeṭas*.
- The term *Ekaveeras* applies to those who have conquered all worldly matters by performing various kind of penances and have realised *Brahmam* and are, therefore, fearless. *Śrī Devī* is served by them.

40. *Ekaprābhava Śālinī* – एकप्राभव शालिनी

- Who is the single most important brilliant ruler (एक = only one, प्राभव = प्रभो: + भाव = प्रभुत्व भाव = rulership)
- प्रभा = Shining or brilliant – *Śrī Devī* is the only brilliant power possessing the unusual quality of protecting the Universe
- *Śrī Devī* shines as the only brilliant ruler of the universe
- *Śrī Devī* is existence absolute and its external manifestation is the Universe.

Ee–ई Series

41. *Eekārarūpā* – ईकाररूपा

- Who has the form of *ee*–ई – the third letter of the *Pancadaśākşarī Mantra*. As per *Soundaryalaharī* (verse 32) *ee* – ई symbolises *Kāma* –काम.
- *'Ĕ'* is the 4th of the 16 vowels in Samskruta. The first letter *A* indicates *Vişṇu*. His sister *Śrī Devī* is indicated by the 4th letter.
- 712th name in *Lalitā Sahasranāma* is *Ee* – ई – One who is in the form of *Ĕ*, the *Kāmakalā* letter. An interesting irony is – this is a single letter name – smallest among the 1000 names – but *Śrī Bhāskararāya* has written longest commentary for this name.

42. *Eeśitrī* – ईशित्री

- Who is the cause of all living creatures
- Who desires discipline or orderliness
- Who rules over everything
- Who establishes everything.

43. *Eepsitārtha Pradāyinī* – ईप्सितार्थ प्रदायिनी

- Who grants whatever possessions (wealth and other things) one desires. (*artha* – अर्थ = wealth).
- *Karma Meemāmsakas* contend that only *Karma* produces the results. This is questionable since *Karma* by itself does not produce results, but it may evoke the giver to grant fruits of *Karma*.
- The below names of *Lalitā* Sahasranāma are comparable here:
  - 63rd name – *Kāmadāyinī* – कामदायिनी – One who fulfills **Her** devotees' desires. Or *Dāyini* – one who gives to **Her** devotees, *Kāma* – *Kāmeśwara*, that is, one who leads **Her** devotees to *Kāmeshwara* and become one with **Him**.
  - 795th name – Kāmadhuk – कामधुक् – One who fulfills all the desires. **She** fulfills all the desires of **Her** devotees.
  - 989th name – *Vānchitārthapradāyinī* – वाञ्छितार्थप्रदायिनी – One who bestows what was sought for by the devotees, in plenty. The devotees need not ask for, just thinking is enough. **She** bestows those things. This is clear from the usage of the word *Vānchita*.

44. *Eeddrugitya Vinirdeśyā* – ईदृगित्यविनिर्देश्या

- Who cannot be determined by evidences such as seeing (*druk* – दृक्) or by any other kind of evidences.
- Who cannot be determined by the usual method of evidence such as by seeing or by perception by any 'sense–organ'
- Who cannot be determined by 'this' or 'that' or 'such' aspect.

45. *Eeśvaratva Vidhāyinī* – ईश्वरत्व विधायिनी

- Who establishes lordship over everything
- Who establishes one–ness with *Eeshvaraḥ* i. e. *Advaita*
- Who grants *Eeshvaratva* or realisation of Eeshvara.
- All these imply one–ness of the universe with *Eeshvara* basis of Monism.

46. *Eeśānādi Brahmamayī* – ईशानादिब्रह्ममयी

- Who is the embodiment (pervades) in Eeshāna and other Brahmas such as *Sadhyojāta, Vāmadeva, Aghora, Tatpuruṣa* and *Eeśāna* – the five Brahmas (सद्योजात, वामदेव, अघोर, तत्पुरुष and ईशान)

47. *Eeśitvādyaṣṭa Siddhidā* – ईशित्वाद्यष्टसिद्धिदा

- Who grants the eight siddhis called as *ashtamāsiddhis. Śrī Devī* grants all these powers or *Siddhis*. The eight *siddhis* are;

Aṇimā – अणिमा	Reducing one's body to the size of an atom and roaming around without being seen by others.
Mahimā – महिमा	Expanding one's body to an infinitely large size
Garimā – गरिमा	Becoming infinitely heavy
Laghimā – लघिमा	Becoming almost weightless
Prāpti – प्राप्ति	Having unrestricted access to all places.
Prākāmya – प्राकाम्य	Getting all desires without any restriction.
Eeśitā – ईशिता	Control of all movable or immovable things.
Vaśitvā – वशित्व	The power to subjugate all.

48. ***Eekşitrī* – ईक्षित्री**

- Who becomes evident (*sākshātkāra* – साक्षात्कार) to those who are indifferent to attachments, that is, who are free from material attachments, who have achieved *gnāna* by becoming indifferent to worldly attachments.
- Who is constantly seeing (or in vigilant about) the entire universe
- Who is an unbiased and detached witness.

49. ***Eekşaṇa Sruşṭāṇḍakoṭiḥ* – ईक्षणसृष्टाण्डकोटिः**

- Who has created and continue to create innumerable universes by just one look or by foresight
- **She** is the cause of the creation of millions of universes by design and foresight (or planning) in the past and in the future.
- 620th name of *Lalitā Sahasranāma, Anekakoṭi Brahmaṇḍa Jananī* – अनेककोटिब्रह्माण्डजननी is worth comparing at this juncture – One who delivered many Crores of worlds. *Virāt, Hiraṇyagarbha* and *Ĕshwara* are the three forms of *Brahmam* created Crores of worlds. **She** is a mother for them also.

50. ***Eeśvara Vallabhā* – ईश्वरवल्लभा**

- Who has *Kāmeshvara* as her consort.
- Who is the object of adoration
- Who has granted power and greatness to *Eeshvaras* such as Brahma, *Vişŋu* and Rudra and has, thus, received their love and regard (respect and adoration).

51. ***Eeḍitā* – ईडिता**

- Who is praised in *Vedantas* – the words of *Vedanta* are in praise of **her**.

52. ***Eeśvarārdhāṅga Śarīrā* – ईश्वरार्धाङ्गशरीरा**

- Who has *Eeshvar* as half of her body
- Who forms the (left) half of the body of Parameshvar
- Whose half body is composed of the body of Eeshvara
- This name can be been interpreted as – **Her** body is in the form of *Ānanda*. The letter *'Ha'* in Samskrutam indicates *Eshvar*. **She** is that half body of *Eeshvar* I.e., **She** is in the form of the letter *'E'* in Samskruta as *Shak*ti *Beeja*.

The letter '*Ha*' can also be wrltten as '*ḥ* -:' (*visarga*). in some schools It is mentioned that **She** is half of it (*Anusvāram*).

- 392nd name of *Lalitā Sahasranāma* – *Śrīkanṭhārdhaśarīriṇī* – श्रीकण्ठार्धशरीरिणी – One who has a body constituting one half of *Śiva*.
- *Brahadāraṇya Upanishad* (verses I–3, 1–4) explains the universal absolute (*Parabrahmam*) becoming two as husband and wlfe; starting from *Ātmaivedamagra Āsīt* till *Sa Imamevātmānam Dvetā'bhātayat Tataḥ*
- It is mentioned in the *Vāyu Purāṇa* as; Lord *Paramaśiva's* body is white in colour whereas his neck is black (on account venom). Similarly, *Śrī Devee*'s body is partly in the form of *Gowree*, which is white in colour and partly in the form of *Kālee*, which is black in colour.
- The 23rd, 34th, 35th and 37th verses from *Soundaryalaharī* talk in the similar lines – *Śarīrārdham Śambhoraparamapi Śanke Hrutamabhūt* I

*Kanch*i *Paramāchārya* in one of his speeches has communicated that in the *Ardhanārīśvara* form the left half belongs to *Shakti* and the right half belongs to *Śiva*. Hence the left half is expected to be red in colour and the right half should be white in colour. But the entire body of *Śrī Devī* is red in colour. And hence arises a doubt in me, that you were not satisfied, by half the body of *Shambu* that he gave and occupied all his body – *Śarīram Tvam Śambhoḥ* I

in a lighter way, *Paramāchārya* said – *Śrī Ādi Śaṇkara* files an allegation on *Śrī Devī* as a thief – while composing *Soundaryalaharī* verses *Śrī Ādi Śaṇkara* closed his eyes and imagined the form of *Śrī Devī*. He expected to see the *Ardhanārīśvara* – half male and half female form. But what he saw was full of female form. That means *Śrī Devī* has stolen the remaining half male form also of *Parameshvara*. Hence, he files an allegation.

53. *Eeśādhi Devatā* – ईशाधि देवता

- **She** is the goddess–divine who is 'above' the *Eesha* (*Eesha* + *adh*i) where *Eesha* stands for both the Almighty and the individual *jeeva* – in the sense that **She** is the substratum that remains after one discard the adjuncts of the *Eeshvara* (almighty) and of the *jeeva* (individual soul). The adjunct of *Eeshvara* is *māyā* and the adjunct of the individual soul is *avidyā*, that is, ignorance. **She** is above (*adhi*) both.
- For whom *Kāmeshvara* is the 'worshipped deity' (meaning **she** is *Parama Pativrata*)
- Who overrides as an attribute-less *Oṃ* who has given up *tat*–तत् (that) symbolised by *Eeshvara* and *tvam* – त्वम् (you) symbolised by *Jeeva* – that means who symbolises truth and is its essence without any qualities.

54. *Eeśvara Preraṇakarī* – ईश्वरप्रेरणकरी

- Who motivates (encourages) *Eeshvara* to perform His duties of creation etc.
- Since **she** is the wife of *Eeshvara,* **she** sees that his orders are carried out properly.

55. *Eeśatāṇḍavasākṣiṇī* – ईशताण्डवसाक्षिणी

- *Śrī Devī* is the witness to the dance of *Eeshvara*
- *Śrī Devī* is watching with enjoyment the manifestation of the activities of the universe as a play
- *Śrī Devī* is the witness to the rhythmical or orderly activities going on in the universe as the *Tāndava* – dance of *Eeshvara*
- Dance involves movements in a rhythmical manner and *Śrī Devī* makes the results of these movements come true – (*sākshātkāra* –साक्षात्कार = manifest in an orderly manner).
- in *Lalitā Sahasranāma* for 232nd name *Maheśvara Mahākalpa Mahā – Tāṇḍava Sākṣiṇī* – महेश्वरमहाकल्प महाताण्डवसाक्षिणी, *Śrī Bhāskararāya* comments as: One who is the witness to the great awesome destructive cosmic dance of Lord *Maheshvarā* at the end of creative cycle.
- The dance by men is called *Tāndavā* and that of women is *lāsya.* It has been mentioned that when *Maheshvara* did the *Tāndavā, Śrī Devī* also did the *Lāsya.* When both are dancing, at the request of *Śrī Devī,* both started the fifth task called *Anugrahā* by re-creating the entire universe with most compassion.
- 41st verse of *Soundaryalaharī* can be compared in this regard;

Tavādhāre Moole Saha Samayayā Lāsyaparayā
Navātmāna Manye Navarasa Mahātāndava Natam I
Ubhābhyā Bhetābhyā Mudaya Vidhi Muddhishya Dayayā
Sanāthābhyām Jagye Janakjananeemat Jagadidam II

I pray in your holy wheel of *Mooladhāra,* you who like to dance and call yourself as *Samaya* and that Lord who performs the great vigorous dance, which has all the shades of nine emotions. This world has you both as parents, because you in your mercy, wed one another, to recreate the world, as the world was destroyed in the grand deluge.

56. *Eeśvarot Saṅga Nilayā* – ईश्वरोत्सङ्गनिलया

- Whose abode is the lap of *Eeshvara* or who sits on the lap of *Eeshvara.*

- Out of 64 offerings to *Śrī Devī*, the 50th one is *Ānantollāsahāsam* – i.e. *Śrī Devī* is pleased with our offerings and seated in the lap of *Śrī Maheshvara* with an attractive and mild smile in her face, to make us happy.
- The 52nd name of *Lalitā* Sahasranāma is *Śivakāmeśvarāngkasthā* – शिवकामेश्वराङ्कस्था, which means – One who sits on the left lap of **Her** consort *Śrī Śivakāmeśvara.*

57. *Eetibādhā Vināśinī* – ईतिबाधाविनाशिनी

- Who destroys the unhappiness (or troubles) caused by fate (destiny) and even animals and people
- Who destroys all troubles caused by calamities.

58. *Eehāvirāhitā* – ईहाविराहिता

- Who is free from all desires because **she** herself is *āptakāma* – आप्तकाम = gets all wishes and desires)

59. *Eeśa Śak*ti – ईशशक्ति

- Who has the strength of *Eeshvara* – such as omniscience, omnipotence and omnipresence.
- **She** is the *shak*ti or power or energy of *Eeshvar.*
- *Parabrahmam* is in the form of *Prakāsā*, the pure luminosity and unrecognisable by all. *Shak*ti makes it recognisable to all, by creating a vibration in it. Thus far unrecognised *Parabrahmam* is able to be identified through motion, quality and actions. **She** is the energy through which the *Parabrahmam* can be identified.

60. *Eeṣat Smitānanā* – ईषत्स्मितानना

- Who has a gentle smiling face (Ever smiling)
- The smile not only adds beauty, but also welcomes and makes It interesting to those who want to reach **Her**.
- The 54th offering out of the 64 is *Ānantollāsa Hāsa Vilāsam Kalpayāmi* – smiling to show the delight.
- *Lalitā Sahasranāma* talks about the smile of *Śrī Devī* in lot many places. To quote a few;
    - 602 – *Darahāsoj Jvalanmukhī* – दरहासोज्ज्वलन्मुखी – One whose face shines with smile.

- 924 – *Darasmera Mukhāmbujā* – दरस्मेरमुखाम्बुजा – One whose lotus face is radiant with a sweet smile.
- The meditation verse also says *Smitamukīm*.

La–ल Series

61. *Lakārarūpā* – लकाररूपा

- *Śrī Devī* has the form of *la*–ल, which is the fourth letter of the *Pancadaśākṣarī Mantra*.
- According to 32nd verse of *Soundaryalaharī*, *La*–ल is root letter (*Bījākṣara*) of Earth.

62. *Lalitā* – **ललिता**

- *Śrī Devī* is very pretty (charming).
- This very hymn is *Lalitā Triśatī* – it will be a surprise, if the name '*Lalitā*' does not appear in the list of 300. The (last but not the least) 1000th name in *Lalitā Sahasranāma* is *Lalitāmbikā* – ललितांबिका for which *Śrī Bhāskararāya* gives a long commentary – a gist is;
  - One who is a beautiful mother called *Lalitā*. Since **She** is the mother of the entire universe, **she** is *Ambikā*. Since **She** is also *Lalitā*, **she** is called as *Lalitāmbikā*.
  - Since **She** is always playing (the tasks like creation, etc., are themselves like sports for **Her**), **She** is called as *Lalitā*.
  - *Padma Purāṇa* says; *Lokānateetya Lalate Lalitā Tena Sochyate* II

in this context the word *Lokā* indicates rays or presiding deities. Controlling all of them, *Śrī Devī* occupies the place *Bindu* with an unexplainable luster. Hence the name *Lalitā*.

63. *Lakṣmī Vāṇī Niṣevitā* – लक्ष्मीवाणी निषेविता

- Who is lovingly served by *Śrī Lakshmee* (embodiment of wealth, beauty and power) and *Śrī Saraswatee* (*Vāni* – embodiment of knowledge *gnāna*). (*Sevitā* = anticipating, with raised eyes).
- It has been mentioned that *Lakshmee* and *Saraswatee* serve *Śrī Devī* on both the sides. A devotee of *Śrī Devī* also becomes merged with *Śrī Devī*. Hence this indicates that *Laskhmee* and *Saraswatee* bless/ serve the devotees of *Śrī Devī* also.

- 614th name of *Lalitā Sahasranāma, Sacāmara Ramā Vāṇī Savya Dakshiṇa Sevitā* – सचामर रमा वाणी सव्य दक्षिण सेविता, says – One who is attended on either side by *Lakshmee* and *Saraswatee* holding *chāmaras* (hand fans).
- in *Soundaryalaharī,* (47th verse) the same meaning is considered;

  Dhanurmanye Savyetarakagruhītam Ratipateḥ
- in *Soundaryalaharī,* (99th verse) also we read:

  Saraswatyā Lakshmyā Vidhihari Sapatno Viharate.

64. *Lākinee* – लाकिनी

- *La*–ल stands for creation and destruction; *aka*–अक indicates unhappiness (*duḥkha* – दुः ख).
- Who sucks away unhappiness and makes the devotees happy
- *Śrī Devī* is the embodiment or has the form of the universe, which has the qualities of being created and destroyed, which appears to be separate from *Brahmam* and appears to be subtle (*Māyā*) and gross.
- Since *Śrī Devī* is the cause of the universe, **she** is also the *Brahmam.*
- *Lā*kinee is the form of *Devee* residing on the *Maṇipoora chakra* and hence represents *Agni* (fire). This is interpreted as one who sucks away the darkness of *ajnāna* (ignorance) and brings in light to the inner conscience. Being fire in essence **She** activates the flow of *Amruta*. Since *Varahi* is the deity in *Maṇipoora Chakra,* which indicates that **she** destroys darkness (*tamas*–तमस्) and illuminates the conscience.
- The names 495 to 503 of *Lalitā Sahasranāma*, gives the complete description and characteristic of *Lākinī* – लाकिनी – this name signifies that which is the fundamental source from which all creation happens, all is sustained and into which all merge, that which shines as the base of all this universe of names and forms.

65. *Lalanārūpā* – ललनारूपा

- Who has the adornments like a woman
- Who has a female form or ornaments like a woman.

66. *Lasaddhāḍimapāṭalā* – लसद्धाडिमपाटला

- Whose body shines the colour of hibiscus and pomegranate i.e. is white and red (Rose) coloured (*la sat*–ल सत् = shines; fits well)

- The red colour of *Śrī Devī* has been mentioned in many names of *Lalitā Triśatī* and *Lalitā Sahasranāma* and in *Soundaryalaharī*. Even in the meditation verse of *Lalitā Sahasranāma* this has been mentioned and repeated here.
- 766th name of *Lalitā Sahasranāma Japāpuṣpa Nibhākrutiḥ* – जपापुष्प निभाकृतिः communicates the same sense – One whose form is like the colour of Hibiscus flower.

67. ***Lalantikā Lasatphālā*** **– ललन्तिका लसत्फाला**

- Who wears on **Her** forehead the ornament called *Lalantika* (made of Pearls surrounding the nine gems)
- Whose forehead shines by the presence of *Lalantika* ornament.
- The forehead of *Śrī Devī* has been described in many a place in *Lalitā Sahasranāma* – names 15, 16, 36, 289, 547, 593, 632, etc.
- 46th verse of *Soundaryalaharī* also describes the beauty of the forehead of *Śrī Devī*.

68. ***Lalāṭanayanārcitā*** **– ललाटनयनार्चिता**

- Who is worshipped by or adored by *Śiva* who has an eye (the third eye) in the centre between the eyebrows – in the centre of the forehead
- Who is worshipped by those sages who pray with their eyes cantered on their foreheads. This is a type of *Mudra* known as *Khecarī Mudra* – खेचरी मुद्रा by which the worshipper fixes his eyes on the centre of his own forehead – this helps the devotee with superficial conscience being dissolved – *Vilīna Citta* – विलीन चित्त and thus he loses his sense perception of the rest of the world during the period when he is in that *Mudra*. *Khecarī mudra* is able to put a person into a state of super–consciousness. Hence this is referred as *Lalāṭa Nayana* by *Mahāyogis*.

69. ***Lakṣanojjvala Divyāṅgī*** **– लक्षनोज्ज्वल दिव्याङ्गी**

- *Śrī Devī* has a divine form with all good qualities (as prescribed in *Sāmudrikā Śāstra*).
- Who shines with all divine qualities.

70. ***Lakṣakoṭyaṇḍa Nāyikā*** **– लक्षकोट्यण्ड नायिका**

- Who lords (or rules) over Lakhs of or Crores of universes. Lakh and Crore mentioned in the name do not exactly mean a lakh or a crore. They mean innumerable.

71. *Lakṣyārthā* – लक्ष्यार्था

- Who is the object of worship (meditation–penance)
- She is the ultimate meaning of all *Vedanta*
- Who is the target of spiritual investigation.

72. *Lakṣṇāgamyā* – लक्ष्णागम्या

- Who is the incomprehensible (cannot be realised or understood) by qualities or attributes
- **She** is unqualified (*lakshaṇa* + *agamyā* – लक्षण + अगम्या) that which is unobtainable.
- *Agamyā* by definitions, called *lakshaṇas*. There are three kinds of *lakshaṇas*:
  - *Jahal–lakshaṇa* is exemplified by "the tea–shop on the Ganges". How can a tea–shop be 'on' the Ganges? Here the word 'Ganges' does not indicate the river Ganges. By context, the word 'Ganges' here only indicates 'the bank of the Ganges'. Thus, the word "tea–shop on the Ganges" simply means "the tea–shop on the banks of the Ganges". Hence the river–meaning of the word Ganges is to be discarded. '*jahat*' means discarded. Hence this is an example of a definition which indicates by discarding.
  - *Ajahal–lakshaṇa* is exemplified by the statement 'white is coming first' in the context of a race of horses, say, where the white horse is coming first. Here the whiteness in the definition is not discarded in the derivation of the meaning. But when we try to understand the relationship between the individual soul (*tvam* = you) and the *Brahmam* (*tat* = Absolute) we cannot have either of these two kinds of definitions; because, the discarding technique of the definition will discard the 'spiritual essence' present in both and the 'non–discarding' definition will take the ignorance of the soul, which is not in *Brahmam* and will also take the creative *māyā* aspect of *Brahmam*, which is not in the individual soul.
  - *Jahad–ajahal–lakshaṇa* — meaning the definition which discards and also not discarded. This means we discard the facets, which are not in both and do not discard the factors which are present in both. This is what we do whenever we say 'That person is the same as the one I saw a few years ago in the mental hospital'. So also, when we say that 'Thou art That' we discard the ignorance aspect of 'thou' and the 'creative' aspect of 'That', but we take into consideration the spiritual content of both and assert that the spiritual content is the same. But even this definition does not describe who 'That' or 'Thou' is.

- Thus, none of the three kinds of definitions 'define' what the Absolute Truth is. Therefore, **she** is unobtainable by definitions!

- 192nd name *Labdhabhaktisulabhā* can also be compared.
- The commentary of *Śrī* Bhāskararāya for the 119th name of *Lalitā Sahasranāma, Bhaktigamyā* – भक्तिगम्या is interesting to note at this juncture: Three interpretations can be made for this name. By true devotion **She** will be present, can be attained and can be recognised.

73. *Labdhakāmā* – लब्धकामा

- Who is endowed with the achievement (realisation) of all desires
- Who has achieved all desires.
- The same message has been conveyed in many a place in this *Triśatī* itself and also in *Lalitā Sahasranāma*

74. *Latātanuḥ* – लतातनुः

- Who has a body like a creeper
- Whose body is ever young like *Kalpa Latā*.
- 34th name of *Lalitā Sahasranāma – Nābhyālavālaromālilatāphala – Kucadvayī* – नाभ्याल वालरोमालि लताफल कुचद्वयी can be compared here – *Śrī Devī*'s two breasts are like fruits of a creeper (line of hair) climbing from the trench (the naval).

75. *Lalāmarājadalikā* – ललामराजदलिका

- Who is adorned (on her forehead) by the mark of *Musk* (*Tilak* of *Kastoori*)
- 16th name of *Lalitā Sahasranāma – Mukhacandrakalangkābha Mruga Nābhi Viśeṣakā* – मुखचन्द्र कलङ्काभ मृगनाभि वेशेषका, for which *Śrī* Bhāskararāya comments as: The *bindi* (musk dot) on the forehead of *Śrī Devī* resembles the black spot on the surface of the Moon and it further beautifies **her** face.

76. *Lambimuktālatāṅcitā* – लम्बिमुक्तालताञ्चिता

- Who is adorned with long garlands of pearls extending to the lower part of the body.

77. *Lambodaraprasūḥ* – लम्बोदरप्रसूः

- Who gave birth to *Ganesha – Lambodara*.

78. *Labhyā* – लभ्या

- Who can be obtained or realised by prayers, listening to prayers or by contemplation.
- Who is not apparent due to nascence (*agnāna* = ignorance) caused by being involved in daily life's activities.
- She is not apparent when one is immersed in worldly activities (*samsāra*), but becomes reflected from people who are involved in prayers.
- The implication is that *Śrī Devī* is obtainable or realisable by contemplation or in company of knowledgeable holy persons.

79. *Lajjāḍhyā* – लज्जाढ्या

- Who is coy (shy) bashful in appearance, or who is sanctified or is auspicious by coyness.
- *Lajja* is modesty. This is one of the righteousness of the inner self. Hence as a sub–character all the righteousness has to be considered. *Ādyā* means one who has such righteousness as form. On account of shyness, people do not show out completely and hide themselves. in the same way, *Śrī Devī* also hides herself with *Tirobhāva* energy and shows up only to her devotees by giving boons.
- 195th name *Lajjapada Samāradhya* – लज्जापद समाराध्या can also be referred.
- 740th name of *Lalitā Sahasranāma* – *Lajjā* – लज्जा says that **she** is in the form of modesty. Shyness (shame or modesty) is an important character of ladies especially *pathivratas*. Scare or fear is also part of it. This is the form of *Śrī Devī*.
- *Saptaśatī* also says;

Yā Devī Sarvabhūteśu Lajjarūpena Samsthitā I
Namstasyai Namstasyai Namstasyai Namonamaḥ II

80. *Layavarjiitā* – लयवर्जिता

- Who is free from destruction or has no destruction
- 143rd name of *Lalitā Sahasranāma*, *Nirupaplavā* – निरुपप्लवा also says that **she** is free from destructions.
- The same meaning is conveyed in 180th name *Nirnāsha* – निर्नाशा.

Hrīm–ह्रीं Series

81. *Hrīmkāra Rūpā* – ह्रींकार रूपा

- Who is in the form of the 5th alphabet of the *Pancadaśākṣarī Mantra* viz. *Hrīm* – ह्रीं.
- This is the *Māyā Bīja* – *a*lso called as *Bhuvaneśvarī Bīja.*
- This Triśatī has 60 names starting with *Hrīm*. Out of these the 99th name just *Hrīm.*
- 301st name of *Lalitā Sahasranāma* – *Hrīmkārī* – ह्रींकारी says one who is in the form of *Hrīm bīja* letters.
    - o *Hrī* means modesty, shyness and bashfulness. One who does this is *Hrīmkārī.*
- Again 302nd name of *Lalitā Sahasranāma* – *Hrīmatī* – ह्रींमती also says – One who has shyness.

82. *Hrīmkāra Nilayā* – ह्रींकार निलया

- Whose abode is *Hrīmkāra* – ह्रींकार.

83. *Hrīmpadapriyā* – ह्रींपदप्रिया

- Who loves the word *Hrīm* – ह्रीं. This alphabet indicates not only power, but also the bestower of all desires
- This word grants all that is aspired for to those who chant *Hrīm* – ह्रीं
- *Śrī Devī* is pleased to occupy the position (*pada* – पद) by which **she** grants all the successes (*Puruṣārthaḥ* – पुरुषार्थः) to those who chant *Hrīm* – ह्रीं.
- *Hrīm* - ह्रीं is composed of *ha* + *ra* + *ee* + *o* – ह + र + ई + (*Anusvāraḥ* –अनुस्वारः) and forms a 'word *mantra'* in itself. *Pada* – पद indicates a status, a position of power.

84. *Hrīmkāra Bījā* – ह्रींकार बीजा

- *Śrī Devī* is identified by the *Bījākṣara* (seed-letter) *Hrīm* – ह्रीं.
- Whose *Bījākṣara* is *Hrīm* – ह्रीं. As the very seed of a Ficus tree (pipal tree) involves – incorporates the potentiality of producing the entire tree, likewise

Hrīm – ह्रीं incorporates the entire universe which is the manifest part of *Śrī Devī*).

85. *Hrīmkāra Mantrā* – ह्रींकार मन्त्रा

- *Śrī Devī* has *Hrīm* – ह्रीं as the *Mantra* for **Her**.
- Whose Mantra is *Hrīmkāra*–ह्रींकार. (*mantra*–मन्त्र – *man*–मन् = mind; *tra*–त्र = protection – This implies that *Śrī Devī* grants protection to those who chant or meditate on *Hrīm* – ह्रीं).

86. *Hrīmkāra Lakṣaṇā* – ह्रींकार लक्षणा

- Who has the character (*Lakshaṇa* – लक्षण) of *Hrīm* – ह्रीं.
- Who has *Hrīm* – ह्रीं as its indicative *lakshaṇa* – लक्षण. There are four letters in the syllable *Hrīm* – ह्रीं. *Ha* – ह्, *Ra* – र्, *Ee* – ई and *M.*
- *Ha* – ह् is the *Ākāsha Beeja* representing sky–ether–space, which is unlimited and indicates *Śiva*. Just as space is uncontaminated or untouched by anything that happens in space, so also the Absolute, which is embedded everywhere in the body is not touched by anything that happens to the body. Hence the *ha* – ह् stands for the Absolute.
- *Ra*–र् represents fire and implies the force needed for functions or action. Hence, *Hra*–ह्र implies unlimited power – power absolute. This letter by fiat of Samskruta grammar always indicates the fiery aspect of the divine, which causes an effect. Hence the *ha* and *ra* together signify the causatively predicated consciousness absolute.
- *Ee* – ई is referred as *manmathabeeja* – मन्मथबीज – the stimulus for action or motivation; and the power of *sthiti* – स्थिति maintenance/ protection lies with *Viṣṇu*. *M* – *Anusvāraḥ* – अनुस्वारः is the indicator of *laya* – लय merging or loss or destruction. The combination of all these characters (qualities) is *Hrīm* – ह्रीं. It implies the cycle of creation, sustenance and destruction aspects for all of which together the source is the Transcendental Absolute Consciousness.
- The three aspects however singly or together do not define the Absolute; but they indicate, point the direction to, the Absolute. Such a defining characteristic is called *tatastha lakshaṇa* – तटस्थ लक्षण, meaning, a 'tentative definition' or 'just an indicative definition'. It is not the final ever–valid definition. Thus, the *Hrīm* – ह्रीं syllable is the *tatastha* – *lakshaṇa* for the Absolute.

- *Shrimad Bhagavad Geeta* 13–32 says: As the all–pervading ether is not tainted, by reasons of its subtlety, to the Self seated in the body everywhere, is also not tainted.

यथा सर्वगतं सौक्ष्म्यादाकाशं नोपलिप्यते । सर्वत्रावस्थितो देहे तथात्मा नोपलिप्यते ॥

Yathā Sarvagatam Soukşmyādākāśam Nopalipyate |
Sarvatrāvasthito Dehe Tathātmā Nopalipyate II

87. *Hrīmkāra Japasuprītā* – ह्रींकार जपसुप्रीता

- Who is pleased by the *japa*–जप (repeated chanting) of *Hrīm* – ह्रीं.

88. *Hrīmmatiḥ* – ह्रींमतिः

- Who is represented by *Hrīm* – ह्रीं.

89. *Hrīm Vibhūṣaṇā* – ह्रीं विभूषणा

- Who is adorned by *Hrīm* - ह्रीं.
- *Ha* – ह् represents whiteness; *Ra* – र represents red (blood red); *Ee* – ई represents blue. Thus, being represented by white, red and blue, **she** also represents *Satva*, *Rajas* and *Tamo Guṇās*. Hence, *Śrī Devī* is also *Māyā*.
- Thus, *Śrī Devī* is referred to as a beautiful damsel adorned with all beautiful qualities.

90. *Hrīm Śīlā* – ह्रीं शीला

- Who has *Hrīm* – ह्रीं as a natural character.
- **She** is by nature *Sacchidananda*, since **she** involves *Brahma*, *Vişŋu* & *Rudra* and *Satva*, Rajas & *Tamas* qualities and also limitlessness.

91. *Hrīmpadārādhyā* – ह्रींपदाराध्या

- Who is meditated upon (worshipped) by word *Hrīm* – ह्रीं.

92. *Hrīm Garbhā* – ह्रीं गर्भा

- Who carries *Hrīm* – ह्रीं in her womb.
- The syllable *Hrīm* – ह्रीं stands for the three divine forms constituting the Trinity – *Brahma, Vişŋu* and *Siva*. These are the three first *Saguna* (with

attributes), as opposed to *Nirguna* (attribute-less) expressions of the Absolute. The respective energies are known as *Vāmā, Jyeshthā* and *Roudree.* The Absolute (the Mother Goddess) has, as it were, all these six in her womb (*Garbha*). That is the reason **she** is *Hrīm Garbhā* – ह्रीं गर्भा.

- in *Śrīmad Bhagavad Geeta* (14–3), Lord Krishna says "my womb is the great *Brahmam*; that I impregnate; then takes place the birth of all beings":

मम योनिर्महद्ब्रह्म तस्मिन्गर्भं दधाम्यहम् । सम्भवः सर्वभूतानां ततो भवति भारत ॥

*Mama Yonirmahadbrahma Tasm*ingarbham *Dadhāmyaham* |
*Sambhavaḥ Sarvabhūtānām Tato Bhava*ti *Bhārata* II

93. *Hrīmpadābhidhā* – ह्रींपदाभिधा

- Who is identified by the *mantra Hrīm* – ह्रीं
- Who is recognised by her position or status by *Hrīm* – ह्रीं.

94. *Hrīmkāra Vācyā* – ह्रींकार वाच्या

- Who is normally called or referred to by the word *Hrīm* – ह्रीं.

95. *Hrīmkāra Pūjyā* – ह्रींकार पूज्या

- Who is worshipped by the *bījākşara* – *Hrīm* – ह्रीं.

96. *Hrīmkāra Pīṭhikā* – ह्रींकार पीठिका

- Whose basis is *Hrīm* – ह्रीं
- For whom *Hrīm* – ह्रीं is the seat.

97. *Hrīmkāra Vedyā* – ह्रींकार वेद्या

- Who can be understood or realised by the *bījākşara Hrīm* - ह्रीं. This understanding or realisation comes through an appropriate *guru* –teacher. It should be noted that it is an 'appropriate *guru*' and not any ordinary *guru*. in this connection the dialogue between Lord Hayagreeva as *guru* and sage Agastya as disciple can be reminded.
- **She** is known by the syllable *Hrīm* – ह्रीं. By nature, **she** is attribute-less. Being attribute-less, **she** cannot be known because to be known would make **Her** an object different from the subject. But the *Hrīm* – ह्रीं syllable when learnt from the *guru* in formal manner and by making it one's own by listening,

probing and meditation, one gets into the bliss of the infinite, which is exactly what **She** is. Thus, what is indirect as the ultimate Absolute becomes direct, through the *Hrīm* – ह्रीं syllable. Hence the name *Hrīmkāra Vedyā* – ह्रींकार वेद्या.

- Lord Krishna's words in *Śrīmad Bhagavad Geeta* (7–14) may be referred in this regard – those who take refuge in me, they alone cross over the illusion of *māyā.* मामेव ये प्रपद्यन्ते मायामेतां तरन्ति ते ।

*Māmeva Ye Prapadyante Māyāmetām Taran*ti *Te* |

98. *Hrīmkāra Cintyā* – ह्रींकार चिन्त्या

- *Śrī Devī* should be meditated upon through *Hrīm* – ह्रीं.
- *Hrīm* – ह्रीं is the same as the *Parabrahma Praṇava Mantra Oṃ* – (*Oṃ aim Hrīm Śrīm Klīm* – ओम् ऐं ह्रीं श्रीं क्लीं). The syllable *Hrīm* – ह्रीं is analogous to the syllable *om*; and thus, it is the means of meditation of *Brahmam*. in both these syllables, the absolute (*parā*) form and the attributed (*aparā*) form of *Brahmam* are indicated. This is an esoteric mystery well–known only by the practitioners of the philosophy of *yoga*. Thus *Hrīm* – ह्रीं contains both the 'facets' of *Brahmam* and naturally it is fit to meditate on the Absolute Mother Goddess by the *Hrīm* – ह्रीं *mantra*.

99. *Hrīm* – ह्रीं

- *Śrī Devī* is the embodiment of the ultimate bliss since **she** carries away or removes all short comings (*ha* – ह = means *Harana* – हरण = carries away). The purport of the syllable, like *Om,* is the blissful state of *Brahmam. Brahmam* is the substratum of everything cognisable by the senses and obtainable by mundane efforts. All these physical things are superimposed on the attribute-less Mother Goddess known as the *Parāshak*ti. Removing the superimposition is itself liberation. By doing this removal, *Hrīm* – ह्रीं reveals itself as the absolute *Brahmam*.
- All energies are attributes of *Śrī Devī*. By disconnecting them we get **Her** liberated form. **She** is seen as a complete liberated goddess. 301st name of *Lalitā Sahasranāma, Hrīmkāree* – ह्रीङ्कारी, says – One who is in the form of *Hrīm beeja* letters.
- in *Swatantra Tantra* it is mentioned as; since *Śrī Devī* takes care of creation, protection and destruction tasks, **she** is called as *Hrīmkāree*.

- *Oṃ* in general is called as *Praṇavam*. This Hrīm – ह्रीं is called as *Śākta Praṇavam*.

100. *Hrīm Śarīriṇī* – ह्रीं शरीरिणी

- Whose body is *Hrīm* – ह्रीं
- Who is embodied in the *Mūlamantra* of *Hrīm* – ह्रीं.
- Out of the 300 names in this *Triśatī* 20 names correspond to each of the letters in *Pancadashee mantra*. It has 60 names corresponding to *Hrīm* – ह्रीं (Annexure 1 & 2 may be referred).
- In *Puruṣa Sūkta* also we read as *Hrīshcha Te Lakshmīśca Patnyou.*

*****

Madhyakūṭam – मध्यकूटम्

Ha – ह Series

101. *Hakārarūpā* – हकाररूपा

- Whose form is *Hakāra* – हकार, which is the sixth alphabet of the *Pancadaśākṣarī Mantra*.
- As per 32nd verse of *Soundaryalaharīee, Ha* – ह is the seed alphabet pertaining to Sun God.

102. *Haladhrutpūjitā* – हलधृत्पूजिता

- Who is worshipped by *Balarāma*, who holds a plough as his weapon.

103. *Hariṇekṣṇā* – हरिणेक्ष्णा

- Who sees like a doe or who looks at many things at the same time
- Whose look expresses vivacity *Cancalatā* – चंचलता and anxiety. The inner meaning being – being concerned with the welfare of **Her** devotees, **she** looks on all sides with concern and anxiety. They are known to be beautiful eyes.
- **She** wants the sympathy and compassion of her sight to fall on all her devotees on all sides and hence her eyes are wavering.
- The below names of *Lalitā Sahasranāma* can be compared:
    - 308 – *Rājīvalocanā* – राजीवलोचना, one whose eyes are like deer, fish and red lotus flower.
    - 561 – *Mrugākṣī* – मृगाक्षी – one who is deer eyed. The eyes of the deer's will not be static at one place – It waves all the sides. This is to escape, in times of danger. Like that of the deer's, the eyes of the high society ladies also will be wavering. This adds to their beauty. Since **She** belongs to the highest class, *Śrī Devī*'s eyes also waves like this.

104. *Harapriyā* – हरप्रिया

- One who is beloved to Lord *Śiva*.
- 409th name of *Lalitā Sahasranāma, Śivapriyā* – शिवप्रिया says that **She** is the beloved of *Śiva.* This implies that **She** is beloved to both *Viṣṇu* and *Śiva*.

105. ***Harārādhyā*** **– हराराध्या**

- Who is worshipped by *Hara* (*Śiva*).
- 406th name of *Lalitā Sahasranāma, Śivārādhyā* – शिवाराध्या also says that **she** is worshipped by *Śiva*.

106. ***Haribrahmendra Vanditā*** **– हरिब्रह्मेन्द्र वन्दिता**

- To whom Hari, Brahma and Indra pay their obeisance – (bow before **Her**). That is, **she** is worshipped by all Gods.
- 627th name of *Lalitā Sahasranāma, Trijagadvandyā* – त्रिजगद्वन्द्या also says that **she** is worshipped by/ in all the three worlds.
- First verse of *Soundaryalaharī* says that **She** is worshipped by the trinity.

107. ***Hayārūḍhāsevitāmghriḥ*** **– हयारूढासेवितांघ्रिः**

- Whose feet are serviced by the God who rides the horse – reference is to *Devendra. Indra* rides on the white horse called *Uccaisravas*, which was got while churning the milky ocean to get nectar.
- *Indra* finds a place among the top worshippers of *Śrīvidyā*. *Śrī Parameshvara, Śrī Hayagreeva, Agastya, Lopāmudra, Kubera*, Sun, Cupid, *Kālidāsa. Manu*, Fire, *Skanda* and *Krodha Bhattarika* (*Durvasa*) are others in the list.

108. ***Hayamedha Samarcitā*** **– हयमेधसमर्चिता**

- Who is worshipped by performing *Ashvamedha Yagna*, which was performed by those kings who had conquered all others on earth.
- Worshipped by those who had obtained all *Purushārtās* by performing the *Ashvamedha yagna* – sacrifice.

109. ***Haryakṣavāhanā*** **– हर्यक्षवाहना**

- Who has lion as vehicle – that is *Durgā* (*hari + aksha*: – हरि अक्षः = Lion).

110. ***Hamsavāhanā*** **– हंसवाहना**

- Who has the Swan as her vehicle – that is *Brahmi*.
- Who has Sun or *Prāna* as vehicle or basis.
- *Hamsa* – हंस has several meanings – Swan, supreme soul, Sun, *Śiva, Viṣṇu, Yogi*, Pure soul (as in *Paramahamsa*)
- *Yashrāyam Purushe Yashrāsāvāditye Sa Ekaḥ* – यश्रायं पुरुषे यश्रासावादित्ये स एकः = that which exists in this man and what exists in the Sun, are same.

- The word *Hamsa*, when derived from the root verb meaning motion (*hanti*) stands for both the Sun and the vital air known as *prāna.* The consciousness that is our essential core has both the Sun and the *prāna* as indicators (*vāhana*) of its manifested omnipresence. Hence, **she** is *Hamsa Vāhanā.*

111. *Hatadānavā* – हतदानवा

- Who killed demons (or *Asura* as or *Dānavās*).
- Assuming various forms of *Shak*ti, **she** killed the *Dānavās* such as *Bhanḍā, Mahishāsura, Shumbha, Nishumbha, Chanḍa, Munḍa, Raktabeeja* and so on. *Saptaśatī* completely deals with this in detail.

112. *Hatyādi Pāpaśamanī* – हत्यादि पापशमनी

- **She** destroys the sins of killing etc.
- **She** protects even those who have incurred sins like committing murder if they seek refuge in Her. **She** destroys all the sins including *Brahmahatti.*
- 31st name *Enaḥ Kūṭa Vināśinī* – एन: कूटविनाशिनी – may also be referred.
- in *Veda* (*Chāndokya Upanishad* IV–24–3) it is mentioned as;

  Yateśikā Tūlamagnou Pradūyataiva Mevāsya Pāpmanaḥ Pradūyante

  Like the point of a reed in the fire, so all the sins are burnt up.
- in *Devī Bhagavatam* also same effect is spoken:

  Chitvā Bhitvā Ca Bhūtāni Hatvā Sarvamidam Jagat I
  Praṇamya Shirasā Devīm Na Sa Pāpair Vilipyate II
  Sarvāvastāgato Vāpi Yuktovā Sarvapātakaiḥ I
  Durgām Druśitvā Naraḥ Pootaḥ Prayāti Paramam Padam II
- in *Brahmaṇḍa Purāṇā*:

  Varṇāsrama Vihīnānām Papishtānām Nrunāmapi I
  Yadrūpa Dhyāna Matrena Dushkrutam Sukrutāyate II

  The sinful actions of those who are devoid of *Varṇa* and *Ashrama* and the wretched also, by mere meditation on *Devee*, become virtuous.

  Śrī Ādi Śaṇkara in his commentary of *Vişṇu Sahasranāma* for the 924th name – *Duşkrutihā* – says – He destroys the bad act of sin or one who does sinful acts.
- Again, for the 992nd name of *Vişŋu Sahasranāma* – *Pāpanāśanaḥ* – **he** destroys the sins in bunches, of those people, who sings hymns in praise of **him**, or worship **him** or meditate upon **him** or just remember **him.**
- The below names of *Lalitā Sahasranāma* deal the same message:

- 167 – *Pāpanāśinī* – पापनाशिनी – One who destroys the sins of devotees. By chanting of **Her** *mantra*, etc., **She** destroys the sins of devotees.
- 555 – *Kalikalmaşanāśinī* – कलिकल्मषनाशिनी – One who is destroyer of sin/ transgression of *Kali.*
- 743 – *Pāpāraṇyadavānalā* – पापारण्यदवानला – One who is like a forest fire that burnt down and destroys all the sins.
- 860 – *Akāntā* – अकान्ता – One who removes sins. *Aka* – sin or sorrow. **She** destroys them. Hence *Akānta.*

113. *Haridaśvādi Sevitā* – हरिदश्वादि सेविता

- Who is served by the Gods who ride a green or yellow horse like Sun and Indra (*Haridaśva* – हरिदश्व means Sun)
- Who is served by Indra, who rides a yellow – green horse and other *Dikpālakās* such as *Indra, Agni, Yama, Nirruti, Varuna, Vāyu, Kubera* and *Eeshāna*).
- The message that **She** is worshipped or served by all Gods has been mentioned in more than one place in this *Triśatī* itself, also in *Lalitā Sahasranāma* and *Soundaryalaharī.*

114. *Hasti Kumbhot Tuṅkakucā* – हस्तिकुम्भोत्तुङ्ककुचा

- Whose breasts resemble the raised humps on the head of the elephant.
- *Soundaryalaharī* verses 7, 72, 73, 74, 75, 77, 78, 79, 80, 93 and 96 describe the beauty of the divine busts of *Śrī Devī.*
- Similarly, right from the meditation verse (*Āpīnavakşoruhām*), names 22, 33, 34 and 36 talks about the beauty of the breasts of *Śrī Devī.*

115. *Hasti Krutti Priyāṅganā* – हस्तिकृत्तिप्रियाङ्गना

- Who is beloved to *Śiva* whose clothes are of the skin of elephant
- Who is the beloved damsel of Him who wears the skin of elephant – that is *Śiva.*
- 409th name in *Lalitā Sahasranāma* – *Śivapriyā* – शिवप्रिया also conveys that **she** is the beloved of *Śiva.*

116. *Haridrā Kuṅkumādigdhā* – हरिद्राकुङ्कुमादिग्धा

- Who is smeared (painted or anointed) with turmeric and vermillion (*Kumkum*).

- 632nd name of *Lalitā Sahasranāma – Sindūratilakāncitā – सिन्दूरतिल*-काञ्चिता says that **she** is adorned with a vermillion mark on the forehead with *Sindooram* (red *Kumkum, Korochan*, etc.).
- *Kumkum* is an auspicious entity for Sumangali ladies. It is given as *prasāda* of *Śrī Devī* to all devotees.

117. *Haryaśvādya Marārcitā* – हर्यश्वाद्यमरार्चिता

- Who is worshipped by *Indra* (who rides a yellow–green horse – *haryashva*) and other *Devas* (Immortals – *Amaraḥ*)
- Such a message is communicated repeated by all the texts just to stress, when such is the case of *Indra* and other *Devas*, how about ordinary people like us – we should also always worship *Śrī Devī*.

118. *Harkeśa Sakhī* – हर्केशसखी

- Who is the lady friend (*sakhee*) of the yellow–haired (Golden coloured) God – that is *Śiva*
- Who is a friend of the God who has hair which have the colour of *Viṣnu*, blue–black hair (*Nīlameghaśyāma* = blue–black as the colour of clouds –i.e. *Viṣŋu*).
- Earlier it was mentioned that **she** is worshipped by Lords *Śiva* and *Viṣŋu* and now it is told that **she** is friend of them. **She** becomes friend to anyone, who worships **her**.

119. *Hādi Vidyā* – हादिविद्या

- Who has the form of the *Mantra* which starts with *Ha* that is, the *Mantra* which was practised by *Lopāmudra* (consort of sage *Agaystya*).
- *Lopāmudra* is one of the top 12 worshippers of *Śrī Vidyā* (and hence *Śrī Devī*). The most famous among the *Pancadashee mantras* are the *Kādi Vidyā* originated by Cupid (starting with the letter '*ka*') and *Hādi Vidyā* originated by *Lopāmudra* (starting with the letter '*ha*'). The method of worship preached by *Lopāmudra* is also called as *Lopāmudrā Vidyā*. Hence this name to *Śrī Devī*.
- 647th name of *Lalitā Sahasranāma, Lopāmudrārcitā* – लोपामुद्रार्चिता says that **She** was worshipped by *Lopāmudra*.

120. *Hālā Madālasā* – हालामदालसा

- Who is happily idle after having become intoxicated by drinking wine (*Madhya*) called *Vāruṇee*.

- *Vāruṇee* refers to *Amruta* which came out during churning of milky ocean. This Amruta (*Sudhārasa*) arising from *Sahasrāra Chakra* goes through the *Sushumna Nāḍi*, which is also referred to as *Vāruṇee*. This perspective finds authority in *Taittreeya Upanishad – Saiṣā Vāruṇī Vidhyā* – सैषा वारुणी विध्या – attaining the final stage during meditation. *Śrī Devī* is in this form. in some places it is mentioned that *Vāruṇee* is made of date fruits.
- in *Lalitā Sahasranāma* also we read as:
  - 333rd name – *Vāruṇī Madavihvalā* – वारुणी मदविह्वला – One who is perturbed by the intoxicating liquor (the wine of spiritual bliss).
  - 575th name – *Mādhvīpānālasā* – माध्वीपानालसा – One who is languid by drinking alcohol.
  - 878th name – *Svātmārāmā* – स्वात्मारामा – One who is rejoicing in herself.
- These names do not imply that *Śrī Devī got* drunk by intoxicating wine. Each has a separate highly philosophical implication.
- Offering alcohol was in vogue in those days, even today for some villages Gods. But this cannot be taken as a general rule. It has to be understood with common sense and in the right sprit.

Sa–स Series

121. *Sakārarūpā* – सकाररूपा

- Who has the form of '*sa*–स' the second letter of the second part (*Kāṇḍa*) of *Pancadaśākṣarī mantra*.
- According to 32nd verse of *Soundaryalaharī, sa* – स is the *bījākṣara* (seed letter) pertaining to Moon (*Chandra* or *Sheeta Kiraṇa*)

122. *Sarvagnā* – सर्वज्ञा

- Who is all knowing – omniscient.
- *Shruti* (*Svetasvatara Upanishad* VI–2) says, omniscient, time of time, possessed of all qualities, all knowing – *Brahmam* is the *Kāla* (death) for *Yama* (god of death) himself; *Gnaḥ Kālakālo Guṇī Sarva Vidyāḥ*
- *Muṇḍako Upanishad* (I–1–9) says; *Yaḥ Sarvagnaḥ Sarva Vit* – one who perceives all and knows all.
- in *Devee Purāṇam* it is said as; *Sarvagna Sarva Vetrutvāt* – As **she** knows everything, **she** is called omniscient.
- We have 196th name of *Lalitā Sahasranāma* as exactly the same.

123. *Sarveśī* – सर्वेशी

- Who causes (stimulates) everything.

124. *Sarvamaṅgalā* – सर्वमङ्गला

- Who is auspicious in all respects
- Who does auspicious effects to all or of all kinds.
- **She** is auspicious by nature. Even unthinking duds, if they resort to any one of the methods of devotion like meditation, recitation, worship, prostration, or ritual *arcanā,* are blessed by **Her** with what they want. Hence, **she** is auspicious even for them.
- Also, **she** is the spiritual core of every being and in that sense, **she** is auspicious Bliss to all.
- Again, the word *Sarva* connotes Lord *Śiva* and to Him, **she** is certainly the most beloved, in fact **She** is half of Him and hence auspicious to Him.
- Also, *Mangala* denotes 'women' and all women are the manifestations of the *Śrī Devī*. The words of *Devee Bhagavatam* as – *Striyās Samastās Sakalā Jagatsu*. She is auspicious to all because women are generally auspicious to all.
- *Śrī Devī* is the *Chit* energy nothing different from *Brahmam*. **She** gives all good fortune to those who satisfy **Her** through meditation, praising through songs and worshipping through *poojas* (even if they are stupid).
- It is wonderful to note that the 200th name in *Lalitā Sahasranāma* is also the same as *Sarvamaṅgalā* – सर्वमङ्गला.
- Again, in *Lalitā Sahasranāma* for the 115th name *Bhadrapriyā* – भद्रप्रिया, *Śrī* Bhāskararāya comments as – One who is fond of everything auspicious.

125. *Sarvakartrī* – सर्वकर्त्री

- Who causes everything.
- For the 53rd name in *Śivā* – शिवा in *Lalitā Sahasranāma, Śrī* Bhāskararāya comments as – Everything ultimately rests with *Śrī Devee*. Hence *Śiva.*
- It is worth noting the 152nd name *Niṣkāraṇā* – निष्कारणा in *Lalitā Sahasranāma,* for which *Śrī* Bhāskararāya comments as *Śrī Devee* **Herself** is the root cause of everything. Hence, **she** has no cause for **Herself**.

126. *Sarvabhartrī* – सर्वभर्त्री

- Who increases (improves) or fills everything.

127. *Sarvahantree* – सर्वहन्त्री

- Who destroys everything.
- The above three names 125 to 127 indicate that **She** is the doer through her *māyā Shak*ti. **She** is the sustainer of everything in the universe. **She** is the destroyer at the time of deluge. Thus, the three names characterise **Her** as the Power behind the three functions of the Trinity.
- *Taitrīya Upanishad* (3–1) also conveys the same as – From which all beings here are born; having been born, by which they remain alive and into which, on departing, they enter.

  Yato Vā Imāni Bhūtāni Jāyante, Yena Jātāni Jīvanti,
  Yat Prayanty Abhisamvişanti

128. *Sanātanā* – सनातना

- Who is ancient; without beginning, eternal.
- in *Shrimad Bhagavat Geeta* (XV–7), Lord Krisha says – an eternal portion of myself having become the soul;

  Mamaivamśo Jīvaloke Jīvabhūtaḥ Sanātanaḥ

129. *Sarvanavadyā* – सर्वनवद्या

- *Śrī Devī* is blameless in every respect
- *Śrī Devī* is desired or wanted by everyone
- *Śrī Devī* is the embodiment of Truth, Knowledge and Bliss in all respects. (*Avadya* – अवद्य means untruth *Anavadya* – अनवद्य is truth – the basic essential truth – *Satyam* – सत्यं)

130. *Sarvāṅga Sundarī* – सर्वाङ्ग सुन्दरी

- **She** is beautiful in all parts of Her body.
- The beauty of *Śrī Devī* has been mentioned in lots of places in *Soundaryalaharī* – in fact, the entire hymn is to describe her beauty only.
- The below names in *Lalitā Sahasranāma* are worth comparing:
  - 241st name – *Chārurūpā* – चारुरूपा – one whose form is exquisite.
  - 562nd name – *Mohinī*– मोहिनी – One who is bewitching/ enchanting.

131. ***Sarvasākṣiṇī*** **– सर्वसाक्षिणी**

- **She** is witness to (or sees) everything
- **She** gives eyes – illumination to everything or regarding everything (*sa* –स + *akshi* – अक्षि = *sākshi* – साक्षि – witness)
- 384th name of *Lalitā Sahasranāma* is *Vişvasākşiṇī* – विश्वसाक्षिणी, which means One who is the witness of everything. *Śrī Devee* sees the entire world.

132. ***Sarvātmikā*** **– सर्वात्मिका**

- **She** is the *Ātma* or soul for all
- **She** is the inner essence of everything.

133. ***Sarva Soukhyadātrī*** **– सर्वसौख्यदात्री**

- **She** gives happiness to all
- **She** grants all kinds of happiness.
- *Soukhya* is happiness. There are four kinds of *Soukhya*: All this are given by **Her** according to the *karma* and *bhak*ti of the individual *jeeva*. Hence, **she** is the giver of all kinds of *soukhya* to all.
  - *Priya*, the feeling of happiness experienced by just seeing the things we want to possess;
  - *Moda*, the feeling experienced when we obtain what we wanted;
  - *Pramoda,* the feeling experienced in the actual enjoyment of the thing we wanted; and
  - *Ānanda*, the holistic experience of Bliss by the experiencer.

134. ***Sarva Vimohinī*** **– सर्व विमोहिनी**

- Who enchants everyone–all
- **She** removes the *Moha*, (delusion), which is the result of ignorance (*agnāna*) of all kinds.
- **She** creates the delusion for all – in the sense that **She** is the *māyā Shak*ti and hence all the false knowledge that get are from **Her**! It has to be noted that this is not said in any derogatory sense. **She** is the substratum of everything and therefore also of the intellect and of the ignorance.
- *Shrimad Bhagavad Geeta* (5–15) says – Knowledge is covered by ignorance; That deludes all beings;

*Ajnānenāvrtam Jnānam Tena Muhyan*ti *Jantavaḥ* |

135. *Sarvādhārā* – सर्वाधारा

- **She** is the basis of everything
- Who is kept in the heart by everyone for worship – *Upāsana*.
- The same name *Sarvādhārā* – सर्वाधारा is found in *Lalitā Sahasranāma* also (659th name), for which *Śrī Bhāskararāya* comments as – *Sarvā* = the whole world, *dhārā* = gradation, i.e., **She** is one with created things. It is called as *Parampara* (race), since everything originates one after another from the previous one.

136. *Sarvagatā* – सर्वगता

- **She** pervades everything.

137. *Sarvāvaguṇa Varjitā* – सर्वावगुणवर्जिता

- Who is free from all bad qualities like *tamas, kāma, krodha, mada, moha, āshcharya,* etc., the six bad qualities.
- *Avaguṇa* is bad qualities, namely those that lead to dishonour, disgrace and disrepute. **She** is devoid of all such qualities.
- Of course, this does not mean to attribute good qualities to the attribute–less *Parāshak*ti. **She** is beyond all qualities. All qualities are those of the mind, which is only a superposition on the substratum of the Absolute. in that sense **She** is not affected by any of them either good or bad. The Space within a jar is not in any way affected by the qualities of the jar. Its relationship to the jar by means of the shape or quality of the jar is a transitory phenomenon.
- *Kato Upanishad* (5–11) says – just as the Sun, which is the eye of the whole world, is not tainted by the colour and external defects, similarly the Self, that is but one, the immanent one, in all beings, is not tainted by the sorrows of the world, it being transcendental;

  Sūryo Yathā Sarvalokasya Cakshuḥ Na Lipyate Cakşuśairbāhya Doşaiḥ |
  Ekastathā Sarvabhūtāntarātmā Na Lipyate Lokadukhena Bāhyaḥ II

138. *Sarvāruṇā* – सर्वारुणा

- **She** is blood–red in colour in all parts of her body.
- This message has been mentioned in many a place in *Lalitā Sahasranāma*. The same name *Sarvāruṇā* – सर्वारुणा itself is found as 49th name.

139. *Sarvamātā* – सर्वमाता

- **She** considers everyone as un–separated from herself

- Who is considered as the cause of all things and action
- Who knows everyone or every thing
- Who considers all in the same way or does not distinguish one from another
- Mother of all
- Right from the very first name of *Lalitā* Sahasranāma as *Śrīmātā* – श्रीमाता – The supreme mother, this has been mentioned in multiple places. Actually, it is a known fact that **she** is the mother of all and no need to mention it anywhere.

140. *Sarva Bhūṣaṇa Bhūṣitā* – सर्वभूषणभूषिता

- **She** is adorned by all types of ornaments & embellishments – qualities
- Since **she** is in everything, **she** has all the ornaments, food and other enjoyments as every other human–being and animal
- Since **she** is in all deities (Gods) **she** is adorned by all devotees in their own manner of their respective deities of choice. Hence, *Śrī Devī* gets all the ornaments from all devotees.
- 51st name of *Lalitā Sahasranāma* – *Sarvābharaṇabhūṣitā* – सर्वाभरणभूषिता, also conveys the same meaning as – one who is adorned with all ornaments.

Ka–क Series

141. *Kakārārthā* – ककारार्था

- *Śrī Devī* is the meaning of the form of '*Ka*–क'.
- As per 32nd verse of *Soundaryalaharī*, *Ka*–क is referred to as seed letter of *Kāmadeva*.
- *Ka*–क represents *Brahma* as per *Shruti* – *Kham Brahma* – कं ब्रह्मा.

142. *Kālahantrī* – कालहन्त्री

- Who destroys Time
- That is, who is beyond Time or transcends time.
- This name occurs in *Lalitā Sahasranāma* also (557th name). **She** destroys, puts an end to, Time (*kāla* = *yama*).
- Time originates from **Her**. Time finally merges in **Her**. Hence, **she** is beyond Time.
- The concept of Time does not apply to **Her**. Hence, **she** destroys Time.

- The word *Kālaḥ* also means the *yama*, the God of death. Hence *kāla*: is Death. Death is what occurs to those who are in the vortex of *samsāra*, the trans–migratory cycle. But those who have crossed the trans–migratory cycle by the Grace of *Śrī Devī* have no business with Death. Thus, **she** conquers Death. When we are unaware of *Śrī Devī*, that much of Time is wastefully spent, that is Time is drained. The more our Time is drained the more we are nearer to Death. Thus, time takes us irrevocably to Death. But those moments of our awareness of the immanent presence of the mother, are conserved moments of Time. Thus saved, the end of our Time is postponed. And those who are aware of Her presence constantly and uninterruptedly conserve all their Time and Death does not approach them! Thus, **she** destroys the 'power' of Time that brings Death nearer.
- There is another aspect of this word *kāla*. The human life is determined by the number of breaths inhaled and exhaled. One inhaling followed by an exhaling is counted as one breath. in the period of 24 hours between one Sunrise to next Sunrise, a human being is supposed to have 21,600 such breaths – which, on calculation, give one breath for every 4 seconds. The more one can reduce this number of 21,600 the longer he lives. That is the reason for *Prāṇāyāma* having a beneficial effect on one's longevity. When we hold the breath inside, the mental aberrations also subside. This is called *Cittavrutti Nirodha,* that is, the stoppage of mind flowing into its channels. When the mind is trained to control its usual flow of thoughts that is the road to total realisation. And that is the time when Time itself stops. The power of consciousness within us, which is nothing but *Śrī Devī* is the prime mover of this achievement, if at all, of ours and in that sense therefore, **she** is the destroyer of Time!
- *Shruti* (*Svetasvatara Upanishad* VI–2) says, omniscient, time of time, possessed of all qualities, all knowing – *Brahmam* is the *Kāla* (death) for *Yama* (God of death) himself; *Gnaḥ Kālakālo Guṇī Sarva Vidyāḥ*

143. *Kāmeśī* – कामेशी

- Who evokes all desires

144. *Kāmitārthadā* – कामितार्थदा

- Who grants all desires.
- in the previous name it was mentioned that **She** evokes the desires and here we read it as **She** satisfies the desires. in this fashion **she** creates the wants in the minds of the devotees and then **she** herself satisfies them.

- 63rd name *Kāmadāyinī* – कामदायिनी of *Lalitā Sahasranāma* also conveys the same meaning as **she** fulfills desires of devotees.
- Again 989th name of *Lalitā Sahasranāma, Vāncitārthapradāyinī* – वाञ्चितार्थप्रदायिनी also communicates the same message – one who bestows what was sought for by the devotees, in plenty. The devotees need not ask for, just thinking is enough. **She** bestows those things. This is clear from the usage of the word *Vānchita*.

145. *Kāma Saṅjīvinī* – कामसञ्जीविनी

- Who brought back Cupid to life (*Manmatha* had been burned by *Eeshvara* earlier).
- in *Lalitā Sahasranāma* also we have the (586th) name as – *Kāmasevitā* – कामसेविता.
- For 62nd name in *Lalitā Sahasranāma* – *Kamakshi* – कामाक्षी, *Śrī* Bhāskararāya comments as – *Kāma* (Cupid) was destroyed by Paramaśiva's third eye and restored to life by *Śrī Devī*'s vision. Hence *Kamakshi*. That is the difference between the sight of father and mother. One destroys and the other creates.

146. *Kalyā* – कल्या

- Who deserved to be meditated upon.
- The same name appears as 903rd name of *Lalitā Sahasranāma* for which *Śrī Bhāskararāya* comments as – one who is skillful in arts. That is the beauty of Samskruta language.

147. *Kaṭhinastana Maṇḍalā* – कठिनस्तन मण्डला

- Whose breasts are firm (hard) and round.
- The beauty of the breasts of *Śrī Devī* has been described in multiple places in various *Shākta* texts.

148. *Karabhoruḥ* – करभोरुः

- Whose thigh is like the trunk of an elephant (*karabha* – करभ also means that part of the hand from the wrist to the little finger).
- The 39th name of *Lalitā Sahasranāma* – *Kāmeśagyātasoubhāgya Mārdavorudvayānvitā* – कामेशग्यात सौभाग्यमार्दवोरुद्वयान्विता, which means – **she** has two beautiful and soft thighs known only to *Śrī Kāmeśwara.*

149. *Kalānāthamukhī* – कलानाथमुखी

- Whose face inspires all the 64 arts – *Kalās*
- Whose face is like the Moon – *kalānātha* – कलानाथा.
- 85th name of *Lalitā Sahasranāma, Śrīmadvāgbhavakūṭaika Svarūpa Mukhapankajā* – श्रीमद्वाग्भव कूटैक स्वरूप मुखपंकजा says that her lotus face represents the *Vāgbhava* group (having 5 syllables), which is the first group in *Pancadaśī.*
- Again 129th name *Lalitā Sahasranāma, Śaraccandranibhānanā* – शरच्चन्द्रनिभानना – one whose face shines like the autumnal Moon, gives pleasure to those who see **Her**.

150. *Kacajitāmbhudā* – कचजिताम्भुदा

- Whose hair put clouds to shame
- The hugeness and weight of **her** hair and braids 'push clouds away'– or 'win over the clouds'– meaning – Her hair expand so much that they push clouds away
- **Her** hair is darker than the clouds.
- 185th name *Lalitā Sahasranāma, Nīlacikurā* – नीलचिकुरा means – one who has shining and beautiful black (blue) hair.

151. *Kaṭākṣasyandi Karuṇā* – कटाक्षस्यन्दि करुणा

- Her eyes (looks) ooze out compassion.
- The thought that the deities, great in all respects, get to protect the indigence in all respects, is called compassion. It is a form of invisible viscera. The taste of sugarcane juice can only be experienced. Similar is the essence of this compassion also – it can be identified through smiling, sweet discussions, benign look of eyes and happy facial expression. Just like the sweet essence was compared to sugarcane juice, this compassion is also compared to liquid. *Syandi Karuṇā* = flood like flowing compassion, *Kaṭākshā* – one who is with the benign look; this means that **She** is with the compassion flooding through Her benign eyes.
- The below names from *Lalitā Sahasranāma* are worth comparison in this regard.
- 326th name – *Karuṇārasa Sāgarā* – करुणारस सागरा – one who is the ocean of compassion as water.

- 581 – *Dayāmūrtiḥ* – दयामूर्तिः – One who is the personification of mercy/ compassion. The thought of very great people to have mercy on the people in distress is called *Karuṇā* (compassion);

Yadyapi Deeneshu Paripālyanābuddhideivānām Mahatām Karuṇetyuchyate.

- 992nd name – *Avyājakaruṇāmūrtḥ* – अव्याजकरुणामूर्तिः – One who has compassion without partiality.

152. *Kapāli Prāṇa Nāyikā* – कपालिप्राणनायिका

- Who reigns over the life of '*Kapāli*'.
- *Ānanda Bhairava* (a form of *Śiva*) carries (bears) a skull (*Kapāla*). Hence, **He** is referred to as '*Kapāli*'.

153. *Kāruṇyavigrahā* – कारुण्यविग्रहा

- Who is the embodiment or personification of compassion (*Karuṇa* made into a statue or idol). Compassion includes kindness, (*dayā* – दया) which is expressed by words, expression of eyes or action.
- Idols, as objects of worship, become necessary because it is impossible to conceive an attribute-less God as *Māyā* comes in the way of conceptualisation of *Nirguṇa* – unqualified – *Brahmam*. Hence, the qualities of kindness, compassion, all–powerfulness, beauty, etc., are projected by the devotees though *Mantras* on a material idol and all kinds of worship are performed to the idol. Hence, idol–worship has to be accepted as a necessary step towards, realisation. This does not contradict the *advaidic* philosophy of identifying the 'self ' and the entire universe with *Brahmam* until the devotee breaks away from *Māyā*. Idol worship is just symbolisation of mental concepts and is a necessary part of worship through *Mantras*.
- Here a form is attributed to the Goddess. It is the form of total compassion and grace. The devotees always need the Grace of the almighty. But if the almighty is taken to be attribute-less, then it may be illogical to expect any activity from that absolute, in the form of a blessing or benefaction. It is absolutely necessary to visualise an attributed God with an active intelligence, which reacts to the sufferings, responds to the prayers and showers its compassion. This is exactly what *Śrī Devī* is. **She** is compassion and grace personified. Grace is part and parcel of **Her**. Grace is **Her** body. That is why when we pray for the Grace of God, we pray to **Her**. Prayer to a personal God should be to a form which comes out of its own free will to create, which

is unbounded by the *karmic* cycle, which is a treasure house of *sat*, *cit* and *Ānanda* and whose sole purpose is to pour out grace. All these constitute the foremost qualities of the mother.

- Earlier described compassion is the beneficence; i.e. the form of inner self. **She** has compassion only as her form (idol). The form is important to give the required boons to the devotees – hence it has been indicated as mind form, a dimension of the inner–self, benign look, smiling words, etc., the body form can be deliberated through these words – compassion is the body of *Śrī Devī*. A body has necessarily been formed for the imagine prone *Brahmam*, whose qualities are; the goal is aiming to create the universe, not bound by any actions, full of awareness bliss, mother's thought aiming only to bless the children, etc. Without such a form the devotees cannot meditate upon. The devotion with form is the basis for devotion without form. That is the reason identification for each of the gods – like *Indra* has the *Vajram* in hand, etc.

154. *Kāntā* – कान्ता

- Who is exceedingly beautiful.
- Who has a captivating beauty.
- The same name *Kāntā* – कान्ता appears in *Lalitā Sahasranāma* also (329th).
- Again in 860th name of *Lalitā Sahasranāma* it has been mentioned as a contradicting name as *Akāntā* – However, it has to be understood as destructor of *Akam* – destructor of sorrow or sin.

155. *Kānti Dhūta Japāvaliḥ* – कान्तिधूतजपावलिः

- Whose lustre or brightness puts to shame to (outshine) the row of hibiscus flowers. (*Japa* + *Āvalī* – जप + आवली = row of *Japākusuma* flowers).

156. *Kalālāpā* – कलालापा

- Who speaks of the 64 *kalās* as a routine matter
- Whose natural language sounds like fine art
- Whose natural language is *Veda shastras*
- Whose speech sounds like a *Kalā* – Music.

157. *Kambukaṇṭhī* – कम्बुकण्ठी

- Whose neck is like a conch with three cross lines. (Accordingly, to *Sāmudrika Sāstrā* the presence of the cross line on the neck is considered to be a sign of beauty in women), that is Her neck is long and has cross lines on it (*kanṭha* – कंठ).

- *Kambukantee* says there are three lines in **Her** neck. The commentary for this describes that these three lines can be compared to the three letters of *Praṇava* as well as *Pashyantee, Madhyamā* and *Vaikharee* speeches.
- 924th name of *Lalitā Sahasranāma, Darasmera Mukhāmbujā* – दरस्मेरमुखाम्बुजा for which *Śrī Bhāskararāya* comments as – *Dara* – conch. Like the stem for Lotus flower, **her** conchlike neck forms the stem of lotuslike face. That neck shines well like conch. It is the practice of poets to compare the neck to a conch.

158. *Karanirjita Pallavā* – करनिर्जितपल्लवा

- *Śrī Devī 's* palm exhibits a posture of divine coquet
- From whose palms (by their posture) sensuousness has been removed
- Who has conquered sensuousness by a posture of her palm

159. *Kalpavallī Samabhujā* – कल्पवल्ली समभुजा

- Whose arms are like the *Kalpa Latā* – the creeper in heaven, which grants all desires.
- 579th name of *Lalitā Sahasranāma, Mruṇālamrududorlatā* – मृणालमृदुदोर्लता, for which *Śrī Bhāskararāya* comments as one whose arms are smooth and slender like a pair of Lotus stalks.

160. *Kastūri Tilakāṅcitā* – कस्तूरि तिलकाञ्चिता

- Whose forehead is adorned (decorated) with a mark of Musk (*Kastoori Tilak*). Ladies are supposed to wear a *tilak* on the forehead and *Kastoori Tilak* is the mark made from musk. This is a traditional Hindu (*Vedic*) custom.
- 16th name of *Lalitā Sahasranāma, Mukhacandrakalangkābha–Mruganābhiviśeṣakā* – मुख चन्द्र कलङ्काभ मृग नाभि विशेषका, can be compared – The *bindi* (musk dot) on the forehead of *Śrī Devī* resembles the black spot on the surface of the Moon and it further beautifies the face.

Ha–ह Series

161. *Hakārārthā* – हकारार्था

- **She** is the essence of the meaning of *Ha*.
- As per 32nd verse of *Soundaryalaharī*, *Ha* – ह is the seed alphabet pertaining to *Ākāsh*/ sky/ space/ ether.
- According to *Soundaryalaharī* (91st verse), *Ha* represents *Hamsa*.
- The *Jnānārnava* says – Oh Parvati! the letter *ha* is in the form of *Bindu* –

  Hakāram Binduroopena Brahmanam Viddhi Pārvati II

162. *Hamsa Gatiḥ* – हंस गतिः

- Whose gait is like that of a swan, which is the vehicle of Lord *Brahma*, slow and graceful who is worshipped by a *Mantra,* which involves well controlled inhale and exaltation. Breath comes out with '*Ha*' and returns with '*Sa*' – *Hakārena Bahiryāti Sakārena Punarvishat.*
- *Ha*–ह represents Sun and *Sa*–स represents Moon. Thus, *Śrī Devī* moves like the Sun and the Moon these representing (personifying) day and night and thus 'Time'. *Śrī Devī* is the ultimate *Moksha* of the *Jeeva*.
- The simplest meaning is – **She** whose gait is lovely and majestic like that of a *Hamsa*, which is the carrier–bird of the creator *Brahma*. But there are several esoteric meanings. The passage of life–giving air in and out of the human body is called *Hamsa*. It goes out by the vocalisation of '*ha*' and comes in by that of '*sa*'. This Hamsa–*mantra* therefore is the constant routine of human life, in spite of its involuntariness. It is called *ajapa–mantra* – where *ajapa* stands for that which is not being chant. **She**, the Mother Goddess, is of this form.
- Also, *Hamsa* denotes the individual soul who gets a body appropriate to the merits and demerits acquired by it in its eternal journey. *Ga*ti is the ultimate destination, of these souls. **She** is the one, who is the ultimate destination of all souls. *Taitreeyopanishad* (2–1) says – *Brahmvidāpnoti Param* – ब्रह्मविदाप्नोति परम् meaning, the one who knows *Brahmam*, reaches the Supreme.
- "From where he never returns" says the scripture in another place – *Yadgatvā Na Nivartante.*
- Also, *Hamsa* denotes a renunciate who has had the enlightenment of the absolute and therefore has no attachment to any particular place or individual. Hence such renunciates roam from place to place. Such are those

who know **Her** as **She** is. Hence, **she** is the one, who is known by such *Hamsa*'s.

163. *Hāṭakā Bharaṇojvalā* – हाटकाभरणोज्वला

- Who is adorned by gold ornaments
- **She** is adorned with *Mangala Sootra* and other ornaments
- **She** is the ornament for the gold–like universe
- Gold represents wealth – thus *Śrī Devī* is the very embodiment of wealth
- *Śrī Devī* shines with wealth as **Her** ornament.

164. *Hārahari Kucābhogā* – हारहरिकुचाभोगा

- Whose round breasts by the beauty and attractiveness, which *Eeshvara* desires to enjoy or steal the *Eeshvaratwa* – the basic qualities of *Eeshvara* (natural qualities) such as self–control or self ever satisfaction and other great qualities,
- The qualities, which adorn *Eeshvara,* are stolen away by **Her** round and beautiful breasts because *Eeshvara* becomes enchanted (and becomes occluded by Māyā.
- The qualities which adorn *Eeshvara* are stolen away – Implying that *Eeshvara* becomes enchanted with the breast of *Śrī Devī* and thus loses His natural qualities.
- The fullness of her breast defeats the *Eeshvaratwa* such as *Tapas* and other qualities of *Hara*. This implies that the beauty of Her breasts enchants *Śiva* so much that his special qualities such as mental concentration, self–control, etc., are overcome and defeated. Hence, *Eeshvara* loses his mental concentration and becomes enchanted by Her full and attractive breasts.
- Whose breasts are adorned by garland of pearls (on appropriate occasions).
- in *Lalitā Sahasranāma*, right from the meditation verse the breasts of *Śrī Devī* has been described in various locations – *Āpīnavakşoruhām* – one who is with big breasts, names 33, 34, 36, etc.
- Similarly, in *Soundaryalaharī* also verses 7, 72, 73, 74, 75, 77, 78, 79, 80, 93 and 96 talk about the breasts of *Śrī Devī*.

165. *Hākinī* – हाकिनी

- Who transgresses (breaks away) limitations (of life and death)
- Who frees (her devotees) from (the limitations of) life and death

- 708th name of *Lalitā Sahasranāma, Sarvopādhivinirmuktā* – सर्वोपाधिविनिर्मुक्ता also says that **She** is devoid of any bases or limitations.

166. *Halyavarjitā* – हल्यवर्जिता

- Who is free from living from the products produced by the plough (*hala*–हल)
- *Śrī Devī* is free from deceptions (*kapaṭa* – कपट) or weaknesses. Since **she** is free from deceptions, **she** embodies the meaning of the phrase *Tatvamasi* – तत्वमसि (you are that) (*hala* – हल = weakness, fault, deception and also plough).

167. *Haritpati Samārādhyā* – हरित्पति समाराध्या

- Who is worshipped by lords of the eight directions (*Dikpālakās*) such as Ind*ra*, *Agni*, *Yama*, *Nirrutti*, *Varuna*, *Vāyu*, *Kubera* and *Eeshāna*).
- **She** has the form of ten directions, says, *Linga Purāṇa*;

Carācharānām Bhūtānām Sarveṣāmavakāśataḥ I
Vyomātmā Bhagavān Devo Bhīma Ityuchyate Budhaiḥ II
Mahāmahimno Dhevasya Bhīmasya Paramātmanaḥ I
Dasha Svaroopā Dig Patnī Sutaḥ Svargashcha Sūribhiḥ II

168. *Haṭhātkāra Hatāsurā* – हठात्कार हतासुरा

- Who quickly destroyed the demons such as *Mahishāsura* and others
- 11th name *Hatadānavā* – हतदानवा may also be referred
- Entire *Saptaśatī* talks about *Śrī Devī* killing all the demons.

169. *Harṣapradā* – हर्षप्रदा

- Who grants joy and happiness.
- 125th name of *Lalitā Sahasranāma* – *Sharmadāyinī* – शर्मदायिनी also says that **she** bestows happiness.

170. *Havirbhoktrī* – हविर्भोक्त्री

- Who devours the offerings at sacrifices.
- *Śrī Devī* assumes the form of *Swāhā Devee* and accepts the offerings made during *Yagnās* and *Yāgās*. (During *Yagna* the offerings are put into fire).
- The 535th name of *Lalitā Sahasranāma* Itself says that she is *Svāhā* – स्वाहा – **she** is in the form of *Svāhā,* the sacred exclamation with which oblations are made in sacrificial fire for gods.

171. ***Hārda Santamasāpahā*** **– हार्द सन्तमसापहा**

- *Śrī Devī* carries away the darkness from the hearts
- **She** removes the darkness of Māyā and grants bliss to her devotees.
- There is darkness (*santamas)* of Ignorance covering up the spiritual center in the heart where the spark of Absolute Consciousness is situated. **She** is the one who dispels (*apahanti*) this darkness. *Hārda* means the heart.

172. ***Hallīsalāsya Santuṣṭā*** **– हल्लीसलास्य सन्तुष्टा**

- *Śrī Devī* is pleased with the group dance of girls with coloured sticks *Ḍandi* dance accompanied by rhythm producing instruments – such as *Mridanga* – by maidens.
- This also indicates that **She** is pleased to see the dance of ladies. **She** is also happy to see a type of dance called *Kolāṭṭam* performed by ladies.
- Earlier in 55th name *Īśatāṇḍavasākṣiṇī* – ईशताण्डवसाक्षिणी – It was mentioned that **she** is pleased to witness the dance of *Eeshvara*.
- 184th name *Lāsya Darśana Santuṣṭā* – लास्य दर्शन सन्तुष्टा - may also be referred.
- 738th name in *Lalitā Sahasranāma, Lāsyapriyā* – लास्यप्रिया clearly mentions that **she** is fond of dancing – either herself or seeing the dance of others.

173. ***Hamsa Mantrārthā Rūpiṇī*** **– हंस मन्त्रार्था रूपिणी**

- *Śrī Devī* is the personification of the meaning of *Hamsa Mantra*; that is the *Praṇava Mantra – Om*, which is chant by great sages (*Parama Hamsās*). It is also called as *Ajapā mantra*.
- *Ham* and *Sa*, which when repeated often sounds like *Sa Aham* I.e. He is I or I am He implied in *Tatvamasi* of *Shruti*.
- **She** personifies in Herself the significance and meaning of the *mantra Hamsa*. The *ha* syllable connotes the word *tat* of the *Upanishads*. The *sa* syllable connotes the word *tvam*. 'That' is not amenable to direct perception. 'You' is direct experience. The *mantra hamsa* contains within Itself the conglomerate Identity of both obtained by what is called the definition, which discards and does not discard – *Jahad Ajahal Lakshaṇa*.
- For the 672nd name of *Lalitā Sahasranāma – Brahmātmaikya Svarūpiṇī* – ब्रह्मात्मैक्य स्वरूपिणी, *Śrī* Bhāskararāya comments as – *ham* indicates the soul and *Sa* indicates the *Parameshwara*. The *Hamsamantra* unites the soul with *Śiva*.

174. *Hānopādāna Nirmuktā* – हानोपादान निर्मुक्ता

- *Śrī Devī* is free from the feelings of rejecting *Hānam* – हानं (unwanted) and desiring (*Upādāna* – उपादान) of what is wanted. The bodiless (*Aśarīra* – अशरीर) *Brahmam* is free from human qualities of desiring or not–wanting – that is *Brahmam* is *Nirmuktvā* – निर्मुक्त्वा = free.

175. *Harṣiṇī* – हर्षिणी

- Who brings joy or evokes happiness (in others).
- 169th name may also be referred.

176. *Hari Sodarī* – हरि सोदरी

- *Śrī Devī* has a common form with Lord *Krishna* – *Hari* – (*Samānam Ekam Udaram* = *sodaree* – समानं एकं उदरं = सोदरी)
- **She** has commonness with *Krishna*, that is same as *Krishna*
- **She** is sister of *Krishna*.
- 280th name of *Lalitā Sahasranāma* – *Padmanābhasahodarī* – पद्मनाभ सहोदरी – One who is a sister of Lord *Viṣṇu* (*Padmanabha*) is worth comparing here.
- in *Saptaśatī* (11–42) *Śrī Devī* herself in her words committed that **She** would be born in the house of *Nandagopā* to *Yashodhā* and shall live in Vindhya mountains:

नन्दगोप गृहे जात यशोदा गर्भ संभवा । ततस्तौ नाशयिष्यामि विन्ध्याचल निवासिनी ॥

Nandagopa Gruhe Jāta Yaśodā Garbha Sambhavā |
Tatastou Nāśayiṣyāmi Vindhyācala Nivāsinī II

177. *Hāhā Hūhū Mukhastutyā* – हाहा हूहू मुखस्तुत्या

- Who has been praised by *Gandharvās* such as Ha Ha and Hoo Hoo. *Gandharvās* are celestial musicians and singers like *Nārada*, *Tumburoo* and others (*stuti* = sing in praise).
- 636th name of *Lalitā Sahasranāma* – *Gandharvasevitā* – गन्धर्व सेविता – also conveys the same message – One who is worshipped by *Gandharvās*, who are celestial musicians.

178. *Hāni Vruddhi Vivarjitā* – हानि वृद्धि विवर्जिता

- **She** is free from (not affected by) decrease or increase.
- This implies that **She** is constant and Immutable or unchanging.

- This also implies that **she** is unqualified (*nirguṇa*).

179. *Hayyaṅgavīna Hrudayā* – हय्यङ्गवीन हृदया

- Whose heart is as soft as butter.

180. *Harigopāruṇāmśukā* – हरिगोपारुणांशुका

- Who is dressed in clothes which are as red as the *Harigopa* insect or worm.
- *Harigopa* is a kind of worm which comes out during the rain in the period of the Sun moving the location of *Ārudra* to *Makha* – (about the latter half of June to the middle of August every year.
- in *Lalitā Sahasranāma*, the 41st name is *Indragopaparikṣiptasmaratū Ṇābhajanghikā* – इन्द्रगोप परिक्षिप्त स्मर तूणाभ जङ्घिका. This is the same as *Harigopa*).

_La_–ल Series

181. *Lakārākhyā* – लकाराख्या

- According to 32nd verse of *Soundaryalaharī*, *La* – ल represents *Devendra* and is the nineth letter of *Pancadaśākṣarī mantra*.
- This Implies that *Śrī Devī* is ever protecting the world by fighting evil just as *Devendra* is always fighting the demons and is thus, protecting the world.

182. *Latāpūjyā* – लतापूज्या

- *Śrī Devī* is worshipped in great devotion and humility by *Parama Pativrata* – परम पतिव्रत (*Latāḥ* – लता:) like *Arundhati* and others, for preserving their *Māngalya*.
- *Kedāra Gowrī* and other special deities are worshipped by flowers and plants.

183. *Layasthiti Udbhaveśvarī* – लयस्थिति उद्भवेश्वरी

- **She** is the root cause (both material and efficient cause) for dissolution (*Laya* – लय), sustenance (*Sthiti* – स्थिति) and birth (*Udbhava* – उद्भव). Anything may be produced from Its efficient cause but it cannot return to that at dissolution unless it is also the material cause. That is why the *Laya* (dissolution) is mentioned here first.
- Who lords over the destruction (*Laya*), preservation (*Sthiti*) and origin

(*Udbhava*) of this world.

- Since destruction or loss is used first, it Implies that the world is without a beginning (*Anādi* – अनादि).

184. *Lāsya Darśana Santuṣṭā* – लास्य दर्शन सन्तुष्टा

- Who is pleased by seeing the dancing by heavenly damsels (to see the enjoyments of her own creations).
- A king, who has got satisfied with all his desires, without aiming at any special fruits, enjoys hunting, games of children, etc. in the same way *Śrī Devī* also enjoys the dance showing four–fold – desirable, undesirable, mixed and abuse and the resultant happiness and sorrow and the consequent facial expressions, the shaking of legs, hands and other organs. Thus, enjoyed *Śrī Devī* bestows the results of the actions of devotees without any partiality;

  Nā Datte Kshyacipāpam Na Chaiva Sukrutam Vibhuḥ
- **She** is pleased with the dance according to the tune and drums performed by *Ramba, Oorvashee* and other *Devata* ladies.
- 55th and 172nd names with related commentaries may be referred.

185. *Lābhā Lābhā Vivarjitā* – लाभालाभा विवर्जिता

- *Śrī Devī* is free from (the feeling of) gain or loss, since **she** is ever contended, **she** is not influenced by gain or loss.

186. *Laṅghyetarāṅā* – लङ्घ्येतराज्ञा

- **She** transcends (or is not under the influence of) the orders or dictates of anyone. The Implication is that **she** is the supreme ruler.
- The *Koorma Purāṇā* says;

  Tvam Hi Yā Paramāshaktiḥ Anantā Parameshtinī I
  Sarvabhedavinirmuktā Sarvabhedavināshinī II
- In the same book in yet another place;

  Shakti Shaktimatorbhedam Vadantyapara Mardhataḥ I
  Abhedam Chānupashyanti Yoginas Tatva Chintakāḥ II

Thou art the supreme *Shak*ti, infinite, supreme ruler, devoid of all differences and the destroyer of all differences.

187. *Lāvaṇya Śālinī* – लावण्य शालिनी

- **She** is in–comparably beautiful.

- **She** is beautiful in all parts (of her body).
- The beauty of *Śrī Devī* is described part by part in *Lalitā Sahasranāma* and *Soundaryalaharī* as well. For instance, for the 218th name *Mahāratiḥ* – महारतिः, *Śrī Bhāskararāya* comments as – *Rati*, wife of Cupid is a most beautiful lady. *Śrī Devī* is more beautiful than *Ra*ti and hence *Mahārati*.
- This can be compared to 46th verse of *Soundaryalaharī* starting with *Lalāṭam Lāvaṇyadvithi Vimalamābhati*.

188. *Laghusiddhidā* – लघुसिद्धिदा

- **She** grants successes (boons) even for simple prayers – even to those who have very little means of worship.
- She grants the eight *Siddhis* to the devotees.
- 47th name with related commentaries can be referred for the names of eight siddhis.

189. *Lākṣārasa Savarṇābhā* – लाक्षारस सवर्णाभा

- Who has the same colour (*savarnā* – सवर्णा) as the colour of lac.
- That Is, **she** is red in colour.
- The red colour of *Śrī Devī* has been mentioned in multiple places in almost all the *Shakta* based texts.

190. *Lakṣmaṇāgraja Pūjitā* – लक्ष्मणाग्रज पूजिता

- Who is worshipped by the elder brother(s) of *Lakshmana* – that is by *Śrī* Rāma and Bharata.
- **She** is worshipped by all sons of Dasharata including Lakshmana.
- *Śrī* Rama installed *Śivalinga* and his consort *Pārvatee* at Rameshvaram and worshipped them. His younger brothers and all his subjects followed the same practice (*agra* – अग्र = leader).

191. *Labhyetarā* – लभ्येतरा

- **She** is the cause for obtaining one's desires such as the four *Purashārthās* – *Dharma*, *Artha*, *Kāma* and *Moksha*.
- Here the word *Labhyā* means that which is obtainable by action motivated by theory of *karma* and *bhak*ti. She is obtainable by these.

- **She** is *Antar Mukha Samārādhyā* (870th name of *Lalitā Sahasranāma* – to be propitiated by an inward perception).
- **She** is also *Bahir Mukha Sudurlabhā* (871st name of *Lalitā Sahasranāma* – not obtainable by external means).

192. *Labdha Bhakti Sulabhā* – लब्ध भक्ति सुलभा

- **She** can be obtained (achieved) easily by devotion or by those who have devotion or concentrated *Bhak*ti.
- *Śrī Ādi Śaṇkara* has given two perspectives;
  - **She** can be easily Identified by those knowledgeable people who have realise *Brahmam* through devotion.
  - **She** will be present to those who have ardent devotion on **Her** without any thought of anything else.
- *Lalitā Sahasranāma* 119th name says – *Bhak*tigamy*ā* – भक्तिगम्या – By true devotion **She** will be present, can be attained and can be recognise.
- Again in 120th name *Bhaktivaśyā* – भक्तिवश्या It has been commented as – One who can be won through true devotion – *Parādeena*.
- Guarantee has been given by Lord Krishna in *Shrimad Bhagavad Geeta* in multiple places:

Yo Mām Pashtati Sarvatra Sarvam Ca Mayi Pashyati
Tasyāham Na Praṅashyāmi Sa Ca Me Na Praṅashyati II (6 – 30)

He who sees me everywhere and sees all in me, he never becomes lost to me, nor do I become lost to him.

Ananyāścintayanto Mām Ye Janāḥ Paryupasate I
Teşam Nityabhiyuktānām Yogakşemam Vahāmyaham II (9 – 22)

To those men who worship me alone, thinking of no other, who are ever devout, I provide gain and security.

193. *Lāṅgalāyudhā* – लाङ्गलायुधा

- **She** bears the plough as the weapon.
- **She** is *Ananta* (never ending) like *Ādisesha* – Implying limitlessness. The plough is the weapon of Lord Balarāma who is the incarnation of *Ādishesha*, who is unending, as mentioned during the churning of Amruta in milky ocean.

194. *Lagnacāmara Hasta Śrī Śāradā Parivījitā* –
लग्नचामर हस्त श्री शारदा परिवीजिता

- *Śrī Devī* is served by *Lakshmi* and *Sharada* who hold in their hands a fan made of yak hair or Lion's mane.
- 63rd name may also be referred.
- *Lalitā Sahasranāma* also says (614th name) *Sachāmararamāvāṇīsavya–Dakṣiṇasevitā* – सचामर रमा वाणी सव्य दक्षिण सेविता – One who is attended on either side by *Lakshmee* and *Saraswati* holding *chāmaras* (hand fans).

195. *Lajjāpada Samārādhyā* – लज्जापद समाराध्या

- *Lajjā* is feeling of remorse and shyness and sense of shame and disgust all these are involved in *Lajja* (also desire and its resulted feeling of shame (due to *Kāmā* – काम).
- The Implication here is that *Śrī Devī* is meditated upon in the mind (in which *Lajja* and *kāma* are natural) and the person becomes remorseful. Such persons also meditate on *Śrī Devī* and get benefited.
- *Lajjā* also means the cycle of life (*Jeeva chakra* – जीवचक्र). This implies that *Śrī Devī* is responsible for the cycle of life – which also includes bliss (*brahmānanda* – ब्रह्मानंद). *Śrī Devī*, who is responsible for the cycle of life, is worshipped for obtaining bliss.
- *Lajja* is the righteousness of inner self. A (character) tool to loathe. All the righteousness has to be considered as sub–characters. With all the righteousness in the inner self, **she** is well worshipped by the inner mind. Amorousness, desire, skeptical doubt, interest, disinterest, help, disturbance, skepticism, indecisiveness and vacillation are all righteousness of inner self. Out of these skepticism means modesty. She is well thought of in these. The below *Veda* statements are evidences of the same:

  *Ya Ātmaṇi Tishtannandaro Yamaya*ti *Guhāhitam Gahvareshtam*
  Purānam Tamātmastam E'nupashyanti Dheerāḥ
- The word *Lajjā* is a *chakra* of soul. in this, for the development of the bliss, which is the presiding form, she is worthy of worship as per the system prevailing in villages.
- 79th and 80th names with commentaries can be referred.

196. *Lampaṭā* – लंपटा

- As per 32nd verse of *Soundaryalaharī*, *La* is the *Bījākṣara* of Earth – now to be considered as the universe. The Implication is that *Śrī Devī* is responsible for the universe (*patā* – पटा = *kāraŋī* – कारणी one who makes, or is responsible for making).
- *Śrī Devī* is vivacious (the dictionary meanings are Lustful, libertine which are applicable) in the sense that *Śrī Devī* has attachment only to *Kāmeshwara*.
- 320th name of *Lalitā Sahasranāma* – *Ramaṇalampaṭā* – रमणलंपटा – one, who is devoted to her husband, is comparable to this name.

197. *Lakuleśvarī* – लकुलेश्वरी

- *Śrī Devī* rules over the destruction the Earth (Universe).
- The world is enveloped in *Māyā* and *Śrī Devī* destroys the *Māyā*
- *Lakula* – लकुल refers to *Swādhiṣṭāna* and *Maṇipoora Chakrās* and *Śrī Devī* is the ruler (*Eeśvarī*) of these. This means that **She** is the *Ātmā* of *Brahmā*, *Viṣnu* and *Rudra*. These are the *grantis* (knots) in the path of the *Kundalinī*.

198. *Labdhamānā* – लब्धमाना

- *Śrī Devī* commands respects (*māna*) from all (including *devas* and humans)
- *Māna* also means *Pooja* (prayer) – hence **she** is the recipient of *pooja* from everyone
- There are four measures namely – *aṇu* – अणु = very small, *mahat* – महत् = very huge, *deergha* – दीर्घ = very long and *hrusva* – ह्रस्व = very short. Hence It can be considered that **She** transcends these four measures.
- **She** cannot be described within these parameters. *Aṇoraṇīyān Mahatomahīyān* – अणोरणीयान् महतोमहीयान् is a description of God – HIs presence in the smallest of small lot and the largest of large lot: God as being qualified and unqualified and also as being limited and unlimited is indicated.
- According to Adavaidic principles, *Paramātmā* and *Jeevātmā* are identical and hence these quallties apply to *Ātma* also.

199. *Labdharasā* – लब्धरसा

- Who is the essence of all *Rasas*;
- *Śrī Devī* is the embodiment of *Ānanda* – bliss.
- *Rasa* is what gives happiness and bliss including like *Ānandarasa*, *Śrungāra Rasa*, *Prīti Rasa*, etc. – all these give happiness.

- 33rd name may also be referred.

200. ***Labdha Sampat Samunnatiḥ*** **– लब्ध संपत् समुन्नतिः**

- *Śrī Devī* is the best and highest since **she** has all the treasures.
- **She** is endowed with *Satyakāmatva* – सत्यकामत्व and *Saccidānandatva* – सच्चिदानन्दत्व and hence, **she** is the highest in all respects and is *Sarvajna* – सर्वज्ञ since **She** is *Brahmam* –

  Eha Nityo Mahimā Brahmanasya – एष नित्यो महिमा ब्रह्मणस्य.

Hrīm **– ह्रीं Series**

201. ***Hrīmkāriṇī*** **– ह्रींकारिणी**

- *Hrīm* – ह्रीं is the last letter of the second *Kāṇḍa* of the *Pancadaśākṣarī mantra*. **She** represents both speech and the speaker.
- Lot many have been spoken relating *Hrīm* – ह्रीं and *Śrī Devī* in this *Triśatī* and all other *Shākta* based texts.

202. ***Hrīmkārādiḥ*** **– ह्रींकारादिः**

- *Śrī Devī* is more ancient than the *Hrīm mantra*. (prior to – *Hrīmkārasya Ādi* – ह्रींकारस्य आदि). The *Vedas* came into being (as a result of) of *Hrīm* and *Śrī Devī* being prior to *Hrīm*, **she** is prior to *Vedas*.
- 296th name of *Lalitā Sahasranāma* can be compared here – *Anādinidhanā* – अनादिनिधना – One who exists without a beginning or end.

203. ***Hrīmmadhyā*** **– ह्रींमध्या**

- **She** is the essence or the core meaning of *Hrīm*.
- *Hrīm* is the active or the central (*Madhya* – मध्य) principle during the period of action and without *Hrīmkārā* – ह्रींकारा there will be no fruit for any prayer or *Karma*.

204. ***Hrīmśikhāmaṇiḥ*** **– ह्रींशिखामणिः**

- Who has *Hrīm* – ह्रीं as the head ornament. Among all ornaments the *Choodāmaṇi* worn on the head is the most precious and Important for ladies. Likewise, among all *Mantras*, *Hrīm* – ह्रीं is the *Shikhāmaṇi*.

- Head ornament is the indicative of possession of great wealth and power. *Śrī Devī* grants all these to those who chant *Hrīm* – ह्रीं. This indicates that *Śrī Devī* has the quallties of the supreme ruler – *Parameśvarī.*
- It can be recollected that Seeta gave her *Chūdāmaṇi* to Anjaneya as an indication, in return to the ring sent by Rāma.

205. *Hrīmkāra Kuṇḍāgni Śikhā* – ह्रींकार कुण्डाग्नि शिखा

- *Śrī Devī* is the flame (head of the fire) or the fire in any *Yagna* – The flame part is the hottest part of the *yagna – Kunda* – (the collection of cinders in the sacrificial fire). It is implied that the hottest part of the fire is at the top of the flame and *Homa* or *Havana* can be successful only If the cinders are aflame, (the *Jvāla* of the *Homakuṇḍa* is implied). To make the fire aflame, Ghee is poured on to the *Yagna kuṇḍ* and *Samits* (pieces of wood from pupil and other trees) are offered to this with appropriate *Mantras. Homa* is ineffective If the flame is not ablaze. (*Upaddīpte[a]gnī Juhoti Mantrairupāsīt* – उपद्दीप्तेऽग्नी जुहोति मंत्रैरुपासीत्).

206. *Hrīmkāra Śaśi Candrikā* – ह्रींकार शशि चन्द्रिका

- *Śrī Devī* is the Moonshine, the beauty (*Candrikā* – चन्द्रिका) of the Moon of *Hrīmkāra.*
- *Chandrikā* implies also the quality of the Moon, namely waning and waxing thereby bringing about the constant change in shape, amount of light and environment. These changes influence life's activities and also living creatures in various ways.
- *Chandrikā* also implies another quality of the Moon – that is giving out *Amruta*. Hence, *Śrī Devī* is the one who grants to the Moon the quality of emitting, oozing out of nectar – *Amruta* – which in turn grants immortality (*amaratva* – अमरत्व) to the *Devas.*
- Likewise, chanting of *Hrīmkāra* – ह्रींकार is like *Amruta* – eternality and Bliss. *Candrika* also implies grace, beauty, peace and comfort.

207. *Hrīmkāra Bhāskara Ruciḥ* – ह्रींकार भास्कर रुचि:

- *Śrī Devī* is the lustre and brightness in the Sun of *Hrīmkāra* – ह्रींकार. *Hrīmkāra* also implies desirability. Sun is ever helpful to the universe/ world and the quality of Sun is due to *Śrī Devī*. Life/ world cannot exist without Sun and this quality and all the quallties are granted by **her**.

208. ***Hrīmkārām Bhoda Caṅcalā*** **– ह्रींकारांभोद चञ्चला**

- *Śrī Devī* is the lightning (*Caṅcalā* – चञ्चला) in the clouds (*Ambhoda* – अंभोद) of *Hrīmkāra* – ह्रींकार. It is implied that the presence of lightning causes the clouds to pour out rain, which in Its turn supports life. Hence lightning is the activator and is responsible for the sustenance of life and this universe.

209. ***Hrīmkāra Kandāṅkurikā*** **– ह्रींकार कन्दाङ्कुरिका**

- *Śrī Devī* is the sprout (germinating part) of the bulb or root (*kanda* – कन्द) of *Hrīmkāra* – ह्रींकार.
- Just as the entire tree with stem, branches, leaves, flowers, fruits and seeds are the result of the first sprout of the seed, so also *Śrī Devī* –the activator, the initiator and the maintainer of the entire universe.
- Also, just as the entire tree is involved in the seed and the bulb, so is *Śrī Devī* is the basic seed of the entire Universe.
- The names 205 onwards till this name, it is conveyed that *Śrī Devī* and the nature are the same – Fire, Moon, Sun, Lightning & clouds and Plants. The entire nature is controlled only by **her**.

210. ***Hrīmkāraika Parāyaṇā*** **– ह्रींकारैक परायणा**

- *Śrī Devī* is the remembrance (one who reminds) that chanting of *Hrīm* – ह्रीं is the only path for the attainment of the four *Purushārthas* – viz, *Dharma*, *Artha*, *Kāma* and *Moksha* (*Parāyaṇā* परायणा = ultimate remembrance).
- From 281 till 300 names may also be referred in this context.

211. ***Hrīmkāra Dīrghikām Hasī*** **– ह्रींकार दीर्घिकां हसी**

- **She** is the female swan in the play pond of *Hrīmkāra*.
- *Hrīmkāra* has been compared to the 'restful–play–pond' (*Deerghikā* – दीर्घिका) for the devotees who have been travelling through the 'forest–of –*Samsāra* (*samsāraṇya* – संसारण्य) and are, therefore, tired. The play pond gives them comfort (*ārām* – आराम्).
- Such a play pond is the abode of the Swan. Swan indicates unlimited comfort. Such a Hamsa is the *Bījākṣara* of *Śrī Devī*.

- 372nd name of *Lalitā Sahasranāma – Bhakta Mānasahamsikā* – भक्त मानस हंसिका can be compared in this regard – One who is in the form of a swan in the lake like minds of the devotees.

212. *Hrīmkārodyāna Kekinī* – ह्रींकारोद्यान केकिनी

- *Śrī Devī* is the peahen (female of peacock) (*morani* – मोरनि) suggesting beauty, attractiveness and music in the garden of *Hrīmkāra*.
- The Peacock is the most beautiful and outstanding (by appearance and voice) among all the creatures living in the forest. Likewise, **she** is the most outstanding among all Gods.

213. *Hrīmkārāraṇya Hariṇī* – ह्रींकारारण्य हरिणी

- **She** is the doe (*harinee* – हरिणी = female deer) in the forest of *Hrīm*.
- The sighting of a doe in the forest dispels fear from the mind of anyone who enters a forest, which may be verminous with wild animals. The first experience of comfort removes fear and encourages the people to enter deeper into the jungle. Likewise, anyone who is a devotee is comforted at the start by *Śrī Devī*.
- *Hrīm* is compared to the jungle through which a devotee has to pass through to achieve *Moksha* and *Śrī Devī* encourages such a person by giving him assurance and courage to pursue through his meditation.

214. *Hrīmkārāvāla Vallarī* – ह्रींकारावाल वल्लरी

- *Āvāla* – आवाल = the little pit dug round the base of a plant for retaining water. *Śrī Devī* is like the creeper (*vallaree* – वल्लरी) coming out of the water retaining pit.
- The Implication is – The water retaining pit is used by people who desire good growth of a plant, which ultimately produces fruits. Likewise, *Hrīm* is the water retaining pit, which should be constantly attended to (watered) by the devotees so that *Śrī Devī* will grant the desired fruits; **She** is compared to the plant or creeper.

215. *Hrīmkāra Pañjara Śukī* – ह्रींकार पञ्जर शुकी

- **She** is the parrot (*shukī* – शुकी) in the cage (*panjara* – पंजर) of *Hrīm*.

- *Śrī Devī* is hidden in *Hrīm* and becomes apparent (evident) only when closely watched – like the parrot in the cage **she** would utter sweet words and blessings when approached.
- From the 212th name she is compared to different animals/ birds – best in that breed – like swan, deer, peahen and parrot and again to lioness later in 217th name.

216. ***Hrīmkārāṅgaṇa Dīpikā* – ह्रींकाराङ्गण दीपिका**

- *Śrī Devī* is the light (*deepikā* – दीपिका) in the resting chamber (*Angana* – अन्गण) of *Hrīm*.
- **She** bestows Illumination to those who enter the *Hrīm* chamber.

217. ***Hrīmkāra Kandarāsimhī* – ह्रींकार कन्दरासिंही**

- *Śrī Devī* is the lioness (*simhee* – सिंही) inside the cave (*kandara* – कन्दर) of *Hrīm*.
- *Kandara* is a cave in the mountain top.
- *Hrīmkāra*, which is referred to in *Vedāntas* is not approachable by ordinary people who are Immersed in worldly enjoyments, just as the cave at the top of the mountain is not approachable by ordinary animals. But a lion can live inside the cage and create fear in the minds of other animals, which, therefore, do not have access to the cave. Only an animal, which has no fear, such as an elephant may dare to enter the cave and in such a case the lion tears up the head of the elephant with his claws with the result pearl and other gems become scattered in the cave (the elephant is supposed to carry a lot of gems in the head).
- Likewise, the fearless man, who does meditate on **her,** gets the benefit of devotion. *Hrīm* is the cave and *Śrī Devī* is the lioness in the metaphor and the persistent devotee is the brave elephant and *Moksha* or freedom or Bliss is the collection of gems coming out of his own head due to the influence and actions of *Śrī Devī*.

218. ***Hrīmkārāmbhoja BhruṅgIkā* – ह्रींकाराम्भोज भृङ्गिका**

- *Hrīm* is the lotus (*kamala* – कमल or *ambuja* – अंबुज) and *bhrungikā* – भृन्गिका is the female bee. *Śrī Devī* is the bee in the lotus of Hrīm.
- *Hrīmkāra* which provides the eight kinds of wealth (*Ashtaishwarya*), eight siddhis and many other desirable qualities is compared to the lotus, which is full of nectar, pollen and other desirable things and *Śrī Devī* is compared to

the bee, which sucks the essential elements in the honey. Hence, those who do *Upāsana* with the *Bījākşara* of *Hrīm* will have the nectar – *Amruta* (honey) – the eight forms of wealth and power due to the benevolence of *Śrī Devī*.

219. *Hrīmkāra Sumanomādhvī* – ह्रींकार सुमनोमाध्वी

- *Śrī Devī* is the sweetness (honey) and fragrance in the flower (*sumana* – सुमन) of *Hrīm*.
- Honey and fragrance in a flower are indicative of its ability to produce fruits. Likewise, *Śrī Devī*, who is sweetness Impersonate can grant fruits to devotees who chant *Hrīm*.

220. *Hrīmkāra Taru Manjarī* – ह्रींकार तरु मंजरी

- *Śrī Devī* is like the cluster of blossoms (*Manjarī* – मंजरी) in the tree (*taru* – तरु) of *Hrīmkāra*.
- Cluster of blossoms suggests the capability of producing many fruits. Likewise, **she** grants many boons to **Her** devotees who pray her with *Hrīmkāra*.

*****

Śaktikūṭam – शक्तिकूटम्

Sa – स Series

221. *Sakārākhyā* – सकाराख्या

- Who is represented by the letter *Sa* or *Śrī Vidyā*
- As per 32nd verse of *Soundaryalaharī Sa* represents *Parā* – the ultimate – as in *Parāśakti* – the ultimate power.

222. *Samarasā* – समरसा

- *Sama* – सम and *rasa* – रस have many meanings *Samarasa* – समरस in the present context would mean – *Śrī Devī* has equal (or is equal to) taste or attachment to all feelings or who is equal to all *Rasās*.
- **She** incorporates within herself all *rasās* – the below table lists down the *rasas*:

#	Name of the *Rasa*		Quality (ies)	Presiding deity	Colour
1.	*Śṛngāram*	श्रृङ्गारं	Love/ attractiveness	*Viṣṇu*	Light green
2.	*Hāsyam*	हास्यं	Laughter/ mIrth/ comedy	*Pramata*	White
3.	*Roudram*	रौद्रं	Fury	*Rudra*	Red
4.	*Kāruṇyam*	कारुण्यं	CompassIon/ mercy	*Yama*	Grey
5.	*Bībhatsam*	बीभत्सं	DIsgust/ aversIon	*Śiva*	Blue
6.	*Bhayānakam*	भयानकं	Horror/ terror	*Kāla*	Black
7.	*Vīram*	वीरं	HeroIc mood	*indra*	Yellow
8.	*Adbhutam*	अद्भुतं	Wonder/ amazement	*Brahma*	Yellow
9.	*Śāntam*	शान्तम्	Peace/ tranquility	*Viṣṇu*	White
10	*Vātsalya*	वात्सल्य	Parental Love		
11	*Bhakti*	भक्ति	Spiritual Devotion		

Note: The last two are additions to the old *Navarasas*.

- *Śrī Devī* is in all *Rasās* equally. The term *Sa* – स indicates *Brahma* (*Shruti* says *Raso Vai Saḥ* – रसो वै स:)
- *Śrī Devī* does not distinguish between the different *rasās*.

223. *Sakalāgama Samstutā* – सकलागम संस्तुता

- *Śrī Devī* is praised or invoked in all kinds of worship
- *Āgamās* – all sacred books (specially works relating to *Śiva* and *Shak*ti) and *Vedas* are considered *Āgamās*.

224. *Sarva Vedānta Tātparya Bhūmiḥ* – सर्व वेदान्त तात्पर्य भूमिः

- *Śrī Devī* is the basis (*Bhūmiḥ* – भूमिः) of the meaning (*Tātparya* – तात्पर्य) of all *Vedāntas*. The *Upanishads* are referred to as *Vedānta* – *Veda* + *Anta* – at the end of the *Vedas* – final essence of *Vedas*. *Śrī Devī* is the subject of all *Vedāntas* – or the very essence of all *Vedāntas*.

225. *Sadasadāśrayā* – सदसदाश्रया

- **She** is the refuge (*Āshraya* – आश्रय) for both *Sat* – सत् = existence and *Asat* – असत् = Non–existence.
- *Sat* includes the three basic elements (*Bhūtāḥ* – भूताः) such as Earth, Water and Fire because these are perceptible by the senses of smell, sight and taste. *Asat* includes remaining two elements air and space, which have no quallties of shape and hence not apparent and can be understood only by the knowledge from other evidences (that is *paroksha jnāna* – परोक्ष ज्ञान). The universe is both *sat* and *asat*. It has no reality of Its own. It appears to be present because of the presence of the substratum namely the Absolute.
- *Śrī Devī* being both *sat* and *asat*, is the basis of all existence (*Sat* + *Asat* (*Tayo*) + *Āshrayā* – सत् + असत् (तयो) + आश्रया).

226. *Sakalā* – सकला

- **She** is associated with fine arts
- The 64 *Kalās* (arts) form the parts of **Her** body
- *Śrī Devī* is the embodiment of the 64 *Kalās*
- The word *Kalā* indicates comfort and happiness. *Śrī Devī* is the personification of comfort and happiness
- **She** represents everything from *Ka* to *La*. The first and the last letters of the *Pancadaśākşarī Mantra* – except for the alphabet *Hrīm*.
- 6th name *Kalāvatī* – कलावती and 149th name *Kalānāthamukhee* – कलानाथमुखी may be referred.

- *Kalā* also means *Tantra*. It has been mentioned in the 31st verse of *Soundaryalaharī* that there are 64 *Tantras*. *Śrī Devī* has all these as **Her** form.

Cautuḥ Şaştya Tantraiḥ Sakalamatisamdhāya Bhuvanam |
Sthitastattat Siddhiprasava Parātantraiḥ Paśupatiḥ II
Punastvannirbandha Dakhila Puruşarthaika Ghatana |
Svatantram Te Tantram Kşititala Mavātitaradidam II

The Lord of all souls, *Pashupat*i, did create the sixty-four *tantras*, each leading to only one desired power and he started his relaxation. But you goaded him mother! – to create in this mortal world, your *tantra* called *Śrī Vidyā,* which grants the devotees, all powers that give powers, over all the states in life.

227. *Saccidānandā* – सच्चिदानन्दा

- *Śrī Devī* represents *sat* – Truth, *chit* – consciousness and *Ananda* – bliss. *Sat* is that, which is not limited by time–past, present and future (*Kālatraya* – कालत्रय), *chit* is self–luminescence that is not dependant on other lights. *Ānanda* is *Brahmam* (*Ānandobrahma Iti Vyajānāt* – आनन्दोब्रह्म इति व्यजानात्) – *Śrī Devī* is the personification of all these.
- 700th name of *Lalitā Sahasranāma* can be compared – *Saccidānanda Rūpiṇī* – सच्चिदानन्द रूपिणी – One who is in the form of *Saccitānanda* – existence, knowledge and bliss absolute.

228. *Sādhyā* – साध्या

- **She** can be practised and achieved (*Sādhitum Yogyā* – साधितुं योग्या)
- *Sādhvī* – साध्वी can be interpreted as consort of *Sādhu* – साधु. *Sādhu* is defined as one who is learned, who has good conduct (*Sadāchāra* – सदाचार.
- *Śrī Devī* is attainable or realisable only by *sadhus*, a person who is learned and has good qualities.
- in some texts this name is written as *Sādhvī* wife of *Sādhu* implying wife of *Sadāśiva*.
- 128th name of *Lalitā Sahasranāma* says *Sādhvī* – साध्वी – One who is paragon of virtue.
- in *Devī Bhagavatam* also it is mentioned as; *Sādhvītyananya Sāmānya Pātivratyena Kīyase*. It is specifically mentioned that *Śrī Devī* did not marry anybody else anytime – any of the incarnations also.

229. *Sadgati Dāyinī* – सद्गति दायिनी

- Who grants *Sadgati* – सद्गति – *Moksha* or freedom – a state from which there is no further return to bondage, the state of eternal happiness and bliss and freedom.
- *Sadgati* = *Moksha, Mukti*, freedom – a state of being with *Brahmam* – *Brahmavidāpnoti Param* – Brahmavid *Brahmaiva Bhavati* – ब्रह्मविद् ब्रह्मैव भवति = knowledge of *Brahmam* makes the person *Brahmam* or association with *Satva guṇās* and *Śrī Devī* grants such a state of being associated with *Satva guṇas*.
- *Śrī Ādi Śaṇkara,* in his commentary says – **She** destroys the Ignorance and gives self–Illuminating bliss.
- 201st name of *Lalitā Sahasranāma Sadgatipradā* – सद्गतिप्रदा – conveys the same message – **She** leads her devotees along the path of salvation. The word *sadgati* means all stages from heaven to *moksha* as per wish of the devotees. **She** gives various stages of liberation as per eligibility.
- *Śrī Ādi Śaṇkara,* in his commentary for *Viṣṇu Sahasranāma,* 699th name *Sadgatiḥ* says; He can be reached by those who understand that the *Brahmam* is the truth. He has elegant, best *Gati* – knowledge.

230. *Sanakādi Munidhyeyā* – सनकादि मुनिध्येया

- **She** is worshipped and meditated upon by *Sanaka* and other sages – *Sanaka, Sanakānanda, Sanātana* and *Sanatkumāra* are the mental sons (*Mānasa Putras*) of Brahmā and they had all the great quallties.
- 726th name of *Lalitā Sahasranāma – Sanakādi Samārādhyā* – सनकादि समाराध्या also communicate the same message as – One who is worshipped by *Sanaka* and others.
- in *Śrī Vidyā* worship, there are three different modes viz, *Samaya, Koula* and *Mishra*. The *Samhitas* of *Sukar, Vashiṣṭar, Sanakar, Sanandanar* and *Sanatkumarar* (jointly called as *Supākāma Pancakam*) follow the *Vaideeka* tradition.
- The four sages *Sanakar, Sanandanar, Sanātanar* and *Sanatkumārar* held *Śrī Devee* in the form of *DakshIṇāmoorthI* in the inner self and initiated by *Śiva*. A surprising scene under the banyan tree – a youth seated as a teacher and advises – the disciples are seniors. Teacher explains in silence and the disciples are relieved of all the doubts;

Chitram Vadataror Mūle Vruddhāḥ Śiṣyāḥ Gurur Yuvā I
Gurostu Mounam Vyākyānam Śiṣyāstu Chinnasamśayāḥ II

231. ***Sadāśiva Kuṭumbinī* – सदाशिव कुटुम्बिनी**

- Who has *Sadāśiva* as her famlly
- Who is the family, (consort of) *Sadāśiva*
- The Implication of all these interpretations is that **she** is an inseparable part of *Sadāśiva*.
- The same name is given as 911th name in *Lalitā Sahasranāma* also – *Sadāśiva Kuṭumbinī* – सदाशिवकुटुंबिनी

232. ***Sakalādhiṣṭāna Rūpā* – सकलाधिष्टान रूपा**

- **She** is the basis of all establishments.
- *Sarva Khalu Idam Brahma* – सर्वं खलु इदं ब्रह्म = everything is indeed *Brahmam*, hence everything is *Śrī Devī*.
- **She** is established by such negatives (*Athāta Neti Neti Neha Nānāsti Kincana* – अथात नेति नेति नेह नानास्ति किंचन). **She** is described in the negative terms such as 'this is not, that is not, etc.'. This is because logically It is not possible to differentiate creation from the creator. It is *agnāna* – अज्ञान, or *Māyā*, which is responsible for this differentiation. Hence, *Śrī Devī* is recognised as the basis for everything.

233. ***Satya Rūpā* – सत्य रूपा**

- **She** is the embodiment of Truth.
- *Sat* indicates *Saccidānanda*, which implies those who can be perceived by one's senses such as the three *Bhootās* – Earth, water and Fire and *asat* represents the unperceivable *Bhootās* such as ether and air. Time is also a non–perceivable unreality, which has effect on existence.
- The same name is given as 818th name in *Lalitā Sahasranāma* also – *Satyarūpā* – सत्यरूपा.

234. ***Samākrutiḥ* – समाकृतिः**

- Who has a perfect proportionate form
- **She** is the personification of all good quallties
- **She** is equal (*samāna* – समान) to *Sadāśiva* in all quallties such as, character, beauty, power, courage, reputation, personality and knowledge (*guṇa*,

soundarya, bala, veerya, yasha, gāmbheerya, jnāna – गुण, सौन्दर्य, बल, वीर्य, यश, गांभीर्य, ज्ञान).

- **She** has unbiased or the same (*samā*) feelings towards all such as the *TrImoortis*.
- **She** has the same quality all the time without the differentiation like childhood, youthfulness and old age *Bālya Youvana Vārdhakta* – बाल्य यौवन वार्धक्त (*Shru*ti and *Smru*ti says – *Samaḥ Sarveṣu Bhūteśu Mad Bhaktim Labhate Parām* – समः सर्वेषु भूतेशु मद् भक्तिं लभते पराम्.

235. *Sarvaprapañca Nirmātrī* – सर्वप्रपञ्च निर्मात्री

- Who is the maker or creator of all worlds
- Who is ever expanding beyond all worlds
- Who creates all the ever-expanding worlds. The concept of ever expansion of the universe is due to our mind exploring the quallties of *Śrī Devī*, who goes beyond the conception of human minds – thereby creating a condition that our mind is incapable of further expansion unless the individual becomes merged *Śrī Devī*.

236. *Samānādhika Varjitā* – समानाधिक वर्जिता

- **She** has no one equal to or above Her. **She** has no equals (*samāna*) or superior (*adhika*).
- Since, **she** is the *Parāshak*ti – the highest power and being *Tripura* (I.e. more ancient than the *TrImoorties* (*Brahmā, Viṣṇu* and *Rudra*) **she** has no equals or superiors.
- *Shru*ti says *Ekāmevādvitīyam Brahma* – एकामेवाद्वितीयं ब्रह्म *Brahmam* is the only one without a second.
- *Smru*ti says *Naitatsamo Adhiko Kuto Anyo Lokatraye* – नैतत्समो अधिको कुतो अन्यो लोकत्रये, *Sam Mānā = Samastebhiḥ Mānā*, सं माना = समस्तेभिः माना– respected by all.
- 809th name in *Lalitā Sahasranāma* – *Parātparā* – परात्परा, says – **she** is the most supreme of the supreme.

237. *Sarvottuṅgā* – सर्वोत्तुङ्गा

- **She** is the highest (*uttumga* – उत्तुंग) of all or greatest of all.
- Since **she** is the cause for everything (all existence), **She** is the greatest, biggest and highest of all and all apparent existence is caused by **Her**.

238. ***Saṅgahīnā*** **– सङ्गहीना**

- **She** is free from attachments or associations because **she** is *Nirāmaya, Niravayavā, Nishkarma* and *Nirguṇa* – hence untouched.

239. ***Saguṇā*** **– सगुणा**

- **She** is qualified
- **She** has all the quallties equally (*samāna guṇāḥ* – समान गुणाः)
- **She** has all good quallties. in some texts this name has been mentioned as *Sadraguṇā* – सद्रगुणा – implying that *Lalitāmba* possess all good quallties. But most used version, mainly *Śrī Ādi Shankara*'s text is *Saguṇā*.
- This may appear contradictory to earlier statement which indicates *NIrguṇatwa*. If dwelt in depth there is no contradiction because the concept of *Śrī Devī* depends on the conceiver and since the conceiver has a limited mind, **she** has to be endowed with quallties. Hence, **she** becomes qualified. The limitation is only in the devotee's mind. When the devotee becomes one with **her**, then **her** qualifications and limitations disappear. That is the reason that both qualified and unqualified *ātmā* is indicated in *Shrut*i. There is really no contradiction and the limitations disappear, therefore, in preaching *Nirguṇa Devī* by worshiping *Saguṇa* deity. This has led to so–called Idol worship. The devotee does not worship the 'Idol' but his own projection of the limitless on the limited Idol and meditates on limitless God. Thus, there is no contradiction between *Bhak*ti and *Gnāna mārgas* – ways and the apparent contradiction among *advaita, dvaita* and *Vishishtādvaita* disappears in a real devotee.

240. ***Sakaleśṭadā*** **– सकलेश्टदा**

- **She** grants all that is desired
- **She** grants to all what they desire
- **She** grants everything to all (*Sakala* + *Iṣṭa* + *Dā*).
- 43rd name *Eepsitārtha Pradāyinī* and 240th name *Sakaleshtadā* may also be referred.
- The same message has been conveyed in *Lalitā Sahasranāma* in 63rd name – *Kāmadāyinī*, 795th name – *Kāmadhuk* and 989th name – *Vānchitārtha Pradāyinī.*
- *Devee Upanishad* also says – *Sā No Mandreshamoorjam Duhānā Dhenur Vāgasmānupasushtotatitu.*

- 4th verse of *Soundaryalaharī* says that **She** bestows more than what was asked or desired; *Tvadanya Pāṇibhyām*.

*Ka–*क Series

241. ***Kakāriṇī*** **– ककारिणी**

- Who personifies *'Ka–*क' – the second letter of the third *Kāṇḍa* or part of *Pancadaśākşarī mantra 'Ka–*क' represents *Māra* or *Manmatha*, as per 32nd verse of *Soundaryalaharī*.

242. ***Kāvya Lolā*** **– काव्य लोला**

- Who enjoys poetry
- She indulges in poetry
- She is pleased with the prayers composed by poets.
- 613th name in *Lalitā Sahasranāma* – *Kāvyālāpavinodinī* – काव्यालोप विनोदिनी – One who gets delighted with poetical speech, dialogue, description, etc.

243. ***Kāmeśvara Manoharā*** **– कामेश्वर मनोहरा**

- Who has won over or captivated or conquered the mind of *Kāmeshvara*.
- 251st name – *Kāmeśvara Manaḥ Priyā* and 253rd name – *Kāmeśwara VImohinī* may also be referred.
- 954th name in *Lalitā Sahasranāma* – *Śambhumohinī* – शम्भु मोहिनी – One who bewitches even *Paramaśiva*.

244. ***Kāmeśvara Prāṇanāḍī*** **– कामेश्वर प्राणनाडी**

- Who is the life pulse (life breath) of *Kāmeśvara*.
- The same is also mentioned in *Lalitā Sahasranāma* as 373rd name.

245. ***Kāmeśotsaṅga Vāsinee*** **– कामेशोत्सङ्ग वासिनी**

- Who resides (sits) on the (left) lap of *Kāmeśvara*.
- 52nd name in *Lalitā Sahasranāma* also says – *Śivakāmeśvarāngkasthā* – शिव कामेश्वराङ्कस्था – One who sits on the left lap of **Her** consort *Śrī Śivakāmeśvara*.

246. ***Kāmeśvarāllṅgatāṅgī*** **– कामेश्वरालिङ्गताङ्गी**

- Whose body is in embrace with *Kāmeśvara*

- Who accepts the embrace of *Kāmeśvara*
- Whose body is in the embrace of *Kāmeśvara*.

247. *Kāmeśvara Sukhapradā* – कामेश्वर सुखप्रदा

- Who gives comfort to *Kāmeśvara*
- Who grants the happiness of the realisation of being *Kāmeśvara* or *Brahmam* or *Saccitānanda* to her devotees.

248. *Kāmeśvara Praṇayinī* – कामेश्वर प्रणयिनी

- Who is loved by *Kāmeśvara*
- Who evokes in *Kāmeśvara* love full submission.

249. *Kāmeśvara Vilāsinī* – कामेश्वर विलासिनी

- Who pleases or entertains *Kāmeśvara*.
- *Vilāsam* means pastime, play, erotic actions, etc. **She** plays with *Kāmeśvara*.

250. *Kāmeśvara Tapaḥ Siddhiḥ* – कामेश्वर तपः सिद्धिः

- Who is the success or fruit of the penance of *Kāmeśvara*.
- **She** did penance and reached *Kāmeśvara*. This has been mentioned in various stories.

251. *Kāmeśvara Manaḥ Priyā* – कामेश्वर मनः प्रिया

- Who is beloved to *Kāmeśvara*.
- The same message is being conveyed in the below names in *Triśatī*; 243 – *Kāmeśwara Manoharā* and 253 – *Kāmeśwara VImohinī*.
- 954th name in *Lalitā* Sahasranāma – *Shambhumohinī* – शंभु मोहिनी – One who bewitches even *Paramaśiva*.

252. *Kāmeśvara Prāṇa Nāthā* – कामेश्वर प्राण नाथा

- Who rules over (or protects) the life of *Kāmeśvara*.

253. *Kāmeśvara Vimohini* – कामेश्वर विमोहिनी

- Who enchants *Kāmeshvara*.

- The same message is being conveyed in the below names in *Triśatī*; 243 – *Kāmeśwara Manoharā* and 251 – *Kāmeśvara Manaḥ Priya.*

254. *Kāmeśvara Brahma Vidyā* – कामेश्वर ब्रह्म विद्या

- Who is the cause of feeling of "being–one–with–*Brahmam*" in *Kāmeśvara.* (*Vidyā* = knowledge) (*Aham Brahmā – Ata Oordvam*).

255. *Kāmeśvara Gruheśvari* – कामेश्वर गृहेश्वरी

- Who is the ruler of the house of *Kāmeśvara*
- Who has *Kāmeśvara* as the ruler of the home.

256. *Kāmeśvara Āhlādakari* – कामेश्वर आह्लादकरी

- Who delights *Kāmeśvara* (*Truptijanyam Sukham*)

257. *Kāmeśvara Maheśvari* – कामेश्वर महेश्वरी

- Who is the great wealth of *Kāmeśvara*
- *Śrī Devī* has great wealth in the form of *Kāmeśvara.*
- A part of *Śrī Ādi Śaṇkara*'s commentary for the – very great, with blemish–less wealth – *Maheśvarī*; *Shruti* says; *Mahatī Ca Sā Eeśvarī Nirupādhikaishvaryavatī, Mahānprabhurvai Puruṣaḥ*"
- 932nd name of *Lalitā Sahasranāma* can also be compared – *Maheśī* – महेशी – One who is the consort of *Maheshvara.*
- The *Devee Purāṇa* says, "As **She** was born from *Mahādeva* and worshipped by great men and as **She** is the consort of *Maheśa*, **she** is called *Maheśī*";

  Mahadevāt Samutpannā Mahadbhir Yata Ādrutā I
  Maheśasya Vadhūryasmānmaheśī Tena Sā Smrutā II

258. *Kāmeśvarī* – कामेश्वरी

- Who is the Goddess worshiped by Cupid
- Who is the ruler of *Kāmeśvara*
- Who is the personification of *Kādi Vidyā* of *Manmatha.*
- 586th name of *Lalitā Sahasranāma* can also be compared – *Kāmasevitā* – कामसेविता – One who was adored by *Kāma* (Cupid).
- in the *Pancadaşī Mantra*, If the repeated letters are removed, nine letters remain. *Tripurā Rahasya* says that *Mahālakşmī* advised Cupid, 108 names, at the rate 12 per letter (9 x 12).

- The *Aruṇopaniṣad* (*Taitrīya Āraṇyam* I–11) says the bodiless son of *Lakshmee,* though without mind, has animation. He got a jewel (*Śrīvidyā*). He, though without fingers, worshipped (folding his hands). Though without neck, he adorned himself with a necklace. Though without tongue, he enjoys taste. Without knowing that taste one should enter the city. When one enters, he should enter after performing secret rites. Secret rites I.e., the knowledge of the essential equality of *Śiva* with *Devee*. The meaning is that worship performed without the knowledge of the essential equality of *Śiva* with *Devee* cannot be effective. This is the vow of *Manmatha*. *Śrī Lakshmeedhara* has given this commentary for the verse:

  Janko Ha Vaidehaḥ I *Aho Rātrais Samājagāma* II
  Putro Nirutyā ValdehaḥI Achetā Yaśca Chetanaḥ II

- 32nd verse of *Soundaryalaharī* starting with *Śivashaktiḥ* also conveys the same sense.
- There are 16 names talking about *Śrī Devī* and *Kāmeśvar* in this *Triśatī* with this name as the last one.

259. *Kāmakoṭi Nilayā* – कामकोटि निलया

- Whose residence is *Kāmakoti*. Among the 96 *Peeṭās* of *Śrī Devī, Kāmako*ti is the most famous being the place of *Śrīchakra*; *Śrīchakra* is her abode.
- *Śrī Ādi Śaṇkara* has interpreted this as residing in *Śrī Chakra*.
- **She** is the *Kāmakoṭi Peeṭa* at *Kāmakoṭṭam* in *Kāncheepuram*.
- **She** is the limit (*koṭi*) of the third wish called *Kāmam* – I.e. **She** is in the form of salvation.
- 589th name of *Lalitā Sahasranāma* can also be compared – *Kāmakoṭikā* – काम कोटिका – One who is in the form of *Kāmakoṭi*.

260. *Kāṅkṣitārthadā* – काङ्क्षितार्थदा

- Who grants all the wealth desired by the devotees.
- It has been commented that **She** bestows whatever asked for by the devotees both in this and the other worlds including the salvation.
- 43rd name – *Ĕpsitārtha Pradāyinī* and 144th name – *Kāmitārthadā* may also be referred.
- Unlike other gods, *Śrī Devee* does not have *Varada* (bestowing boons) *mudra*. No need for It. *Śrī Ādi Śaṇkara,* in his commentary for the 4th verse of *Soundaryalaharī* mentions as – **Her** Lotus feet Itself bestows more than what is sought for, by the devotees;

Tvadanyaḥ Pānibhyām Abhayavarado Daivataganaḥ
Tvamekā NaIvāsi Prakatita Varābheetyabhinayā I
Bhayāt Trātum Dātum PhalamapI Cha Vānchāsamathikam
Sharanye Lokānām Tava Hi Charaṇāveva Nipunou II

- 989th name of *Lalitā Sahasranāma* can also be compared – *Vānchitārthapradāyinī* – वाञ्छितार्थ प्रदायिनी – One who bestows what was sought for by the devotees, in plenty.

La–ल Series

261. *Lakāriṇī* – लकारिणी

- *Śrī Devī* has the form of *La*, which is the third letter of third *Kāṇḍa* of *Pancadaśākşarī Mantra.*
- As per 32nd verse of *Soundaryalaharī, 'La'* is the *Bījākşara* – root alphabet pertaining to *Hari.*

262. *Labdha Rūpā* – लब्ध रूपा

- **She** has all good quallties (*Roopā* – beautiful)
- **She** has the form (body) with all good quallties
- **She** has both, qualified (*Saguṇa*) and unqualified (*Nirguṇa*) forms.

263. *Labdhadhī* – लब्धधी

- **She** has knowledge of all things – omniscient.

264. *Labdha Vāṅcitā* – लब्ध वाञ्चिता

- **She** has all that is desired (*Vāṅcitā*) *Ishtakāma.*

265. *Labdapāpa Manodūrā* – लब्दपाप मनोदूरा

- **She** is far away (inconceivable/ unattainable) from the minds of sinners or those who do actions not approved by *Vedas.*

266. *Labdhāhamkāra Durgamā* – लब्धाहंकार दुर्गमा

- Who is beyond the reach of arrogant people. The Implication is that people, who have *ahankāra* due to *rajas* and *tamas* actions, cannot realise *Śrī Devī.*
- Only *sattva* qualities are necessary for the mind to concentrate and control sensuousness; and without such self–control and mental concentration, it is

not possible to conceive the *saguṇatva* and *nirguṇatva* of *Śrī Devī*. *Ahankār* produces *Māyā* and *Māyā* prevents concentration.

267. *Labdha Śaktiḥ* – लब्ध शक्तिः

- **She** is all powerful or **she** has all powers.

268. *Labdha Dehā* – लब्ध देहा

- **She** acquires a body or form as **she** pleases – The quality of a shape or body is like the 'Solid Ghee', which can also lose Its shape when warmed. This Implies that **she** is with form as well as is formless.

269. *Labdhaiśvarya Samunnatiḥ* – लब्धैश्वर्य समुन्नतिः

- Who has limitless or incalculable wealth.
- This implies that **she** can also grant incalculable amount of wealth to her devotees.

270. *Labdha Vruddhiḥ* – लब्ध वृद्धिः

- **She** is ever expanding, ever growing and limitless.
- *Cāndokya Upanishad* (VII–24–1) says – where no other thing is seen, no other thing is heard and no other thing is identified that is limitless. However, where anything else is seen or heard or identified that is small; that which is limitless is eternal.

271. *Labdha Līlā* – लब्ध लीला

- **She**, by her playfulness, makes others happy.
- 340th name of *Lalitā Sahasranāma* says – *Vilāsinī* – विलासिनी – **She** is playful, showing the same thing in different forms.

272. *Labdha Youvana Śāl*inī – लब्ध यौवन शालिनी

- **She** is ever youthful, ever–young *ajaram, amrutam, abhayam, Brahma* – Implying ever powerful and who always grants hope to devotees. There are three states (*avasthā*) – namely infancy, youth (Implying growth), old–age – *bālya youvana vārdhakta* – बाल्य यौवन वार्धक्त or sense which anticipates the end or death when all hope is lost.

- Youthfulness (*youvana*) Implies power, progress and hope.
- 430th name of *Lalitā Sahasranāma* also – *Nityayouvanā* – नित्ययौवना – says that **She** is eternally young. **She** is juvenile and youthful without any growth or deterioration.

273. *Labdhātiśaya Sarvāṅga Soundaryā* – लब्धातिशय सर्वाङ्ग सौन्दर्या

- **She** has great beauty in all the parts of the body and personality
- *Veda* says *Sarvamanohara Moorti, Na Tasya Pratimāsti.*
- 972nd name of *Lalitā Sahasranāma* says that **she** is always and everywhere beautiful – *Āśobhanā* – आशोभना
- The second part of *Soundaryalaharī* (verses 42 to 100) is entirely devoted to describe the beauty of *Śrī Devī.*

274. *Labdha Vibhramā* – लब्ध विभ्रमा

- Who has the capacity to enchant by her child– like– playfulness.

275. *Labdha Rāgā* – लब्ध रागा

- Who has all feelings – *Rāgas* – *Veda* says *So Kāmayata.*
- *Rāga* also means fervent longing. *Śāṇḍilya Sūtra* mentions as; *Dveṣa Pratipakṣā Bhāvādrasa Śabdācca Rāga* – since without hatred and also It is mentioned as essence – the *Śrī Devī* is beyond all these and **She** has no object for longing.

276. *Labdha Patiḥ* – लब्ध पतिः

- Who has obtained her husband by her own desire (*svayamvara*).

277. *Labdha Nānāgama Sthitiḥ* – लब्ध नानागम स्थितिः

- **She** has the form (appearance) as per various forms of worship.
- **She** has been established by various *Āgamas* – *vedic* rites
- *Śrī Devī* has been prescribed by various *Karmas'* as with different rules (*Āgamas*).
- **She** maintains the different *Vedas* (*Agama* is used here in this sense) which proclaim the three methods of spiritual upliftment, namely, *karma, upāsanā* (*bhak*ti) and *jnāna*. **She** maintains them not only during the period of manifestation of the absolute but also during those periods of non–manifestation. Further **She** observes the *Vedic* regulations like the *pātivratya*

dharma in tune with the Lord Krishna's declaration: Should I not ever engage myself in action, without relaxation, men would in every way follow My Path. These worlds would perish, if I did not perform action; *Shrimad Bhagavad Geeta*; 3–23, 24

Yadi Hyaham Na Varteyam Jātu Karmaṇyatandritaḥ |
Mama Vartmānuvartante Manuşyāḥ Pārtha Sarvaşaḥ ||
Utsīdeyurlme Lokā Na Kuryām Karma Cedaham ||

278. *Labdha Bhogā* – लब्ध भोगा

- **She** has all kinds of pleasures.

279. *Labdha Sukhā* – लब्ध सुखा

- Who has every happiness.
- From whom all kinds of happiness can be obtained.
- 408th name of *Lalitā Sahasranāma* says that dispenses happiness/ auspiciousness – *Śivankarī* – शिवंकरी

280. *Labdha Harśābhi Pūritā* – लब्ध हर्शाभि पूरिता

- *Śrī Devī* is full of joy.
- **She** is the refuge of all happiness.
- 60th name – *Eshatsmitānanā* can also be referred.
- 924th name of *Lalitā Sahasranāma* – *Darasmeramukhāmbujā* – दरस्मेर मुखांबुजा – also says that **her** lotus face is radiant with a sweet smile.
- 9th verse of *Soundaryalaharī* also says that **she** is fond of joy (the union of *Śiva* and *Shak*ti);

Mahīm Mūlādhare Kamapi Maṇipūre Hutavaham
Sthitam Svādhişṭāne Hrudhi Marutamākāśamupari |
Manopi Bhrumadye Sakalamapi Bhitvā Kulapatham
Sahasrare Padme Saha Rahasi Patyā Viharase ||

Hrīm – ह्रीं **Series**

281. *Hrīmkāra Mūrtiḥ* – ह्रींकार मूर्तिः

- *Śrī Devī* is the embodiment of *Hrīm* – **her** form is of *Hrīm*.

- Lot many has been talked about *Śrī Devī* and *Hrīm* mantra in this *Triśatī* and all other Shākta based texts.

282. *Hrīmkāra Soudha Śruṅga Kapotikā* – ह्रींकार सौध शृङ्ग कपोतिका

- **She** is the female dove in the peak (*shrunga*) of the tower of the mansion (*soudha*) of *Hrīm*
- *Ha* in *Hrīm* is white in colour and is compared to the tower or peak; *Ra* in *Hrīm* is amber or brick–red and hence resembles the walls, *Ee* is the peak of the tower and *m* is the central *Bindu* representing *Śrī Devī* – female pigeon– dove is ever alert and hence **She** is compared.

283. *Hrīmkāra Dugdhābdhi Sudhā* – ह्रींकार दुग्धाब्धि सुधा

- *Śrī Devī* is the nectar in the milky ocean.
- *Dugdha* implies that it has been pressed out by hand from the breast or udder. *Abdh*I is the ocean surrounding the earth as in *Āpa Dhīyante Asmin* – water has the quality of giving life in this world. The ocean, which is compared to the milk in the breast, giving life to the child, which presses the breast for the milk. in *Hrīm* also because of the association with *hakāra* It represents the whiteness of the milk.
- *Dugdhasya Abdhi* = ocean of milk. The Implication is that the Devotees gets the milk by practising prayers – by efforts including all the processes – like a child gets Its life-giving milk.

284. *Hrīmkāra Kamalendirā* – ह्रींकार कमलेन्दिरा

- *Śrī Devī* is *Indira – Lakshmi* in the Lotus *Kamala* of *Hrīm*.
- The comparison of *Hrīm* to Lotus is because lotus has not only pleasant smell but beauty and attractiveness. Being on the lotus implies that *Śrī Devī* grants all the *Purushārthās – Dharma, Artha, Kāma* and *Moksha*.

285. *Hrīmkāra Maṇi Dīpārcciḥ* – **ह्रींकार मणि दीपार्च्चिः**

- **She** is the light–flame in the lamp of the gems (*Maṇidvīpa*).
- *Maṇidvīpa* is the lamp, which is never extinguished because it is not troubled by air or breeze and *Śrī Devī* is the *Prakāsh* (Illumination).
- The Implication is that **she** grants Illumination (*Gnāna*) eternally to those who meditate on *Hrīm*.

286. *Hrīmkāra Taruśārikā* – ह्रींकार तरुशारिका

- The word *taru* – means a tree. It is derived from *Tārayati* – saves or protects from falling (and also means helps crossing of ocean) any person who climbs the tree for fruits.
- *Shārika* is a pretty bird (with yellow–red eyes, face and feet), which not only able to speak human language but tell the past, present and future and thereby help a person. *Śrī Devī* is compared to this bird – *Śārika* – which prevents a human being from falling (from the fruit bearing tree) and committing sin and utters him the words of the *Veda* and grants him all fortunes (fruits) and thus be good;
- *Śrī Devī* is the *Shārika* bird on the tree of *Hrīm.*

287. *Hrīmkāra Peṭakamaṇiḥ* – ह्रींकार पेटकमणिः

- *Śrī Devī* is the gem (*maṇi*) – inside a safe box of *Hrīm.*
- *Hrīm* is compared to a box and *Śrī Devī* is the gem inside the box
- *Peṭak* also means a collection of gems and *maṇi* is a diamond.
- The implication is that *Śrī Devī*, being a diamond outshines all others in the collection of gems.

288. *Hrīmkāra Darśa Bimbitā* – ह्रींकार दर्श बिम्बिता

- *Śrī Devī* is the reflection in the mirror of *Hrīmkāra.*
- *Ādarsha* also means 'an example' and *Śrī Devī* is the example to reflect all the great attributes and truths (embodied in *Vedānta*) without any blemish.
- *Śrī Devī* is the reality reflected in *Hrīm.*

289. *Hrīmkāra Kośāsilatā* – ह्रींकार कोशासिलता

- *Śrī Devī* is the great sword (hidden) inside the scabbard sheath of *Hrīm.*
- The Implication is that the sword protects people from enemies who cause miseries. **She** removes the cause of miseries. The sword is hidden inside the sheath when not in use.

290. *Hrīmkārasthāna Nartakī* – ह्रींकारस्थान नर्तकी

- *Śrī Devī* is the danseuse on the stage of *Hrīm.*
- Dance is an art involving movement of eyes, lips, rhythmical movement of arms, hands and feet on the ground accompanied by music. **She** is presented

as danseuse since **she** not only enchants by exhibiting various movements and actions, but also exhibits her capacity to destroy the evil people or protect the good people, as the situation warrants.

291. *Hrīmkāra Śuktikā Muktā Maṇi* – ह्रींकार शुक्तिका मुक्ता मणि

- *Śrī Devī* is the pearl inside the oyster of *Hrīm*.
- During the period of *Swāti* constellation in the human calendar (approximately during last week of October to the first week of November for 12 to 13 days) rain drops are supposed to fall into the oyster in the sea and they are supposed to convert the drops into pearls.
- Also, rain drops are pure. Likewise, *Śrī Devī* is pure *sattva* and incorporated in *Hrīm* and expressed on pure *Triguṇa*, such as *sattva*, *rajas* and *tamas*.
- This implies that oyster is the necessary medium to obtain pearls. Similarly, *Hrīm* is necessary to achieve **her**. Oyster is the apparent vehicle for pearl and *Hrīm* is the apparent vehicle for achieving *Śrī Devī*.

292. *Hrīmkāra Bodhitā* – ह्रींकार बोधिता

- *Śrī Devī* is *Hrīm* and *Hrīm* is *Śrī Devī*.
- A cognate object is perceived by the senses and this becomes knowledge. Hence, knowledge is the result of physical perception by senses and action. Likewise, true *Brahmam* is perceived through *Karma*. Knowledge is self–evident and does not need previous experience for remembering. *Hrīm*. Likewise, it is the root *mantra* and is the sense perceived form of *Śrī Devī*.
- *Ha*, *Ra*, *Ee* and *m* are the perceptible forms of *Hrīm* and lend themselves to different meanings and connotations. Together (that is *Hrīm*) It represents *Mahā Tripura Sundarī*.
- Hence, **she** is addressed as *advaita*, single and no–two – *Shruti* says:

  Eka Eva Tu Bhūtātmā Bhūtebhūte Vyavasthitaḥ

  – one exists in all forms of existence.
- *Ekadhā Bahudhā Caiva Druśyan*ti *Jalacandravat* – although there is only one Moon, it appears as many in the reflections in water. All these Illustrations and similes Imply that there is only one existence, but it is reflected in different objects – *ekam sat* = one Truth.

293. *Hrīmkāramayasouvarṇa Stambhavidruma Putrikā* –
ह्रींकारमयसौवर्ण स्तंभविद्रुम पुत्रिका

- *Śrī Devī* is like the coral Icon (Idol) in the golden pillar of *Hrīmkāra*
- **She** is the coral Icon in the hall of *Hrīm* supported by golden pillars

- **She** is the main deity occurring as a coral Idol in the hall called *Hrīm* supported by golden pillars.

294. *Hrīmkāra Vedopaniśad* – ह्रींकार वेदोपनिशद्

- *Śrī Devī* is the *Upanishad* (ultimate essence) of the *Veda* of *Hrīm*.
- Here *Hrīm* is compared to the *Vedas* and *Śrī Devī* is mentioned as the final part or essence or ultimate philosophy of the *Vedas* the *Upanishads*.
- *Veda* means knowledge of all things and the *Upanishads* are an end part of the *Vedas* or the philosophical meanings of the *Vedas*. *Śrī Devī* is like the *Upanishad*, that Is, *Brahmam*.
- The four *Vedas* are divided each into 3 parts – namely *Karma Kāṇḍa, Upāsanā Kāṇḍa* and *Gnāna Kāṇḍa*. *Karma* and *Upāsanā* are necessary and are prescribed for achieving *gnāna*. But only *Karma* and *Upāsanā* lead to *tamas* (darkness) and are objected to, since these are intended only to get benefits of this world. Only the pursuit of *gnāna* leads to freedom or *Moksha*. *Advaita gnāna* – (namely, knowledge of one–ness) is what the *Upanishads* expound. *Śrī Devī* is like the *Upanishads* (knowledge of *advaita*) for the *Vedas*, which have *Karma* and *Upāsanā*.
- Further, *up* indicates closeness or nearness. That which reveals closeness to *Brahmam* is *Upanishad*. *NI* is an adjective – meaning sitting, obtaining and end. Hence *Upanishad* implies sitting near or next to *Brahmam* after being rid of *agyāna* – Ignorance – the realisation that *Jeeva* gets absorbed ultimately into *Brahmam*. Hence *Upanishad* finally means *Brahma Vidyā*.
- Etymologically, *Upanishad* means sitting close to a teacher and practically, it signifies a frank discussion between the teacher and the student to remove Ignorance by realising the supreme Brahmam. Hence, *Upanishads* are speculative and logical studies of the end part of the *Vedās* – *Upanishads* form a religion–philosophical discussion – beyond the region of only *Karma* and *Upāsana*.
- **She** is the *Upanishad* for the *Veda* that is the very syllable *Hrīm*. This syllable stands for the *Śrī Devī*. The *Vedas* stand for the Transcendental Absolute. This is indicated by the *Upanishads*. *Upa* means proximity. By the proximity of *māyā* with the Absolute, the latter is taken to be the attributed almighty and that is reflected in the minds as the soul. Hence the soul indicated by the word *upa* rids Itself of the adjunct of Ignorance and becomes the absolute Itself. This is the very meaning of *Upanishad*.

- In other words, the *jeeva,* the individual soul, recognises Itself to be the absolute. Thus, the term *Upanishad* connotes the absolute Itself. The syllable *Hrīm* is the *Veda* that takes us to the absolute.

295. *Hrīmkāradhvara Dakṣiṇā* – ह्रींकारध्वर दक्षिणा

- *Śrī Devī* is like the *Dakshiṇā*, what is given to the priests or preceptor after the *yagna* which is *Hrīm*.
- *Śrī Devī* is the fruit of the *Yagna*. Any *yagna* (sacrificial rite) can bear fruit only If the priests are given *Dakshiṇā*. Hence, the word *Dakshiṇā* indicates getting the fruits of being a priest or *Ritviks*. *Śrī Devī* Ii, therefore, the fruit (result) of the *Yagna*, which is *Hrīm*. (No spiritual ritual can be successful without the sanctification from the wife also – *Mukhasya Dakshiṇā Patnee*).
- As per *Vedic* rules, the wife of the person who performs the *Yagna* has to grant her sanctions If the *Yagna* has to bear fruits. For the *Japa Yagna* of *Hrīmkāra*, *Śrī Devī* is the *Dakshina* or the *Phala* – the result or the fruit. *Dakshiṇā* is Important for the success of the *Yagna* – (*Pradhāna Dakshiṇā Mukham*).
- Offering or sacrifice of money is Itself *Yagna – Devatoddeshena Dravyatyāgo Yāgaḥ – Tyakta Dravyasya Agnou Prekshepo Homaḥ – Rutviguddeshena Vedyāmarthevibhāgo Dakshiṇā.* All these words of *Vedas* Imply the Importance of *Dakshiṇā* after the performance of the religious rites.
- There are four kinds of offerings during a *Yagna*.
    - First *havis* is offered directly to fire either with the material, which is to be offered or by putting dried *samit* (wooden pieces as prescribed for each deity).
    - Second – *Dakshiṇā* is given to the priest (preceptor) who conducts the performance of the Yagna.
    - Thirdly, *dāna* given to the people who have assembled in the *Yagna Shāla* and
    - Lastly *Bhikshā* (alms) given to those outside the *yagna shāla* and begging. The performer of the *yagna* (*karta*) has to grant all these to the best of his ability and the quantity cannot be prescribed nor demanded by any of the recipients. As per *Vedas*, the recipients should bless the performer of the *yagna*.
- Mythologically – *Dakshiṇā* was a beautiful daughter of *Viṣṇu* who offered her to *Brahma*. *Brahma* in turn offered her to *Yagneshvar* (fire–God) who married her. They had a son whose name was *Phala*.

Śrī Devī Bhāgavata Part I

296. *Hrīmkāra Nandanārāma Navakalpakavallarī* – ह्रींकार नन्दनाराम नवकल्पकवल्लरी

- *Śrī Devī* is like the *Kalpa* creeper in the pleasant resting bower (green house) in the garden in *Indraloka*. The garden in *Indraloka* is called *Nandanārāma,* since It gives pleasure and is restful.
- *Śrī Devī* is referred to as resting in the bower (Green house) of *Kalpa Latā*, which grants everything that is asked for to those who meditate on *Hrīm*.

297. *Hrīmkāra Himavad Gaṅgā* – ह्रींकार हिमवद् गङ्गा

- *Śrī Devī* is the Ganga in the snow mountain (Himalayas) of *Hrīm*.
- Ganga is the sacred river from Himalaya carrying coolness and comfort. Hence, **she** is compared to Ganga.
- 450th name of *Lalitā* Sahasranāma says that **she** is in the form of river Ganges – *Nandinī* – नंदिनी.

298. *Hrīmkārārṇava Koustubhā* – ह्रींकारार्णव कौस्तुभा

- *Śrī Devī* is like the *Koustubha Maṇi* in the ocean of *Hrīmkāra*.
- *Koustubha* is the most precious and the most beautiful among the 14 gems, which came out when the mIlky ocean was churned for nectar and is self–luminescent and this is worn by *Viṣṇu* who embodies Immense wealth, great beauty and other qualIties. Likewise, those who indulge in the *japa* of *Hrīm* (meditate on *Hrīm*) obtain the status of *Lakshmeepatitva* (ruler–ship over all wealth) and one–ness with *Viṣṇu*.
- *Śrī Neelakaṇṭa Deekshitar* in his book called *Neelakaṇṭa Vijaya* says that – The left part of *Ĕshwar* in the form of a lady, sometimes seen as male having *Kamalā* as his consort and wearing the *Koustuba* gem in his heart. What is the difference in this? Same supreme being. in one sense mother of universe (*Jaganmātā*) and in another sense the *TrIvIkrama* form measuring all the three worlds.

299. *Hrīmkāra Mantra Sarvasyā* – ह्रींकार मन्त्र सर्वस्या

- *Śrī Devī* is the embodiment of everything in the Mantra of *Hrīm* – all–powerfulness and Immense possessions.

300. ***Hrīmkāra Para Soukhyadā*** **– ह्रींकार पर सौख्यदा**

- *Śrī Devī* grants highest happiness and comfort to those who meditate on *Hrīm.*
- *Śrī Devī* grants Immeasurable happiness *Parasoukhya.*
- *Śrī Devī* grants eternal happiness – happiness of being one with *Brahmam* (*Parabrahmam*) – (*Brahmagnānāpnoti Param*).
- Happiness of being one with *Brahmam* (*Parabrahmam*) is becoming one with *Brahmam* (*Vignānāpnoti Param* – knowledge of *Brahmam* makes a person attain *Parabrahmatva* and *Brahmaveda Brahmaiva Bhavati.*
- *Brahmam* is *sat, chit* and *ānanda*. **She** gives happiness and satisfaction to those who are intent on the meditation or recitation of *Hrīm*. This happiness comes out of the benefaction by the Absolute of all the four goals of life, namely, *dharma, artha, kāma* and *moksha.*
- Another meaning Is: **She** gives holistic (*para*) happiness as against the individual happiness associated with the divinities *Brahma, Viṣṇu* and *Rudra.* This is usually referred to as the consummate integrated bliss.
- *Lalitā Triśatī* has 60 names corresponding to *Hrīm*. Each of the groups ends with 20 names starting with *Hrīm*. This shows the significance of the *Hrīm mantra*. Let all the devotee's worship with *Hrīm mantra* and get benefitted.

इति श्री ललिता त्रिशती स्तोत्रम् सम्पूर्णम्

Iti *Śrī Lalitā Triśatī Stotram Sampūrnam*

Thus, *Śrī Lalitā Triśatī Stotram* is complete.

Oṃ Tat Sat

*****

Śrī Lalitā Triśatī

उत्तर भागः *Uttara Bhāgaḥ* (End part)

Phalaśruti (The fruits or results)

The *phalashruti* of every hymn based on a particular God/ Goddess will talk high about that God and the results mentioned will sometimes be a kind of exaggeration – crores of years of life, etc. This should not be taken in literal sense. The intention is – by chanting the hymn the worshipper will get lot of benefits – also there are lots of procedures to chant a hymn – in *Śrīmad Bhagavad Geeta* Lord Krishna says *Ananyā Cintayanto Mām* – without thinking of anyone/ anything else, If anyone worships me! – does the devotee worship with that type of focused mind. Also by talking high about one God does not under estimate the power of other Gods. This is just to increase the faith of the devotees. Definitely hymns on every God are powerful – some may be powerful at some occasions and some other for particular wish. Hence they should not be taken as literally.

The *phalashruti* of *Śrī Lalitā Sahasranāma* completely gives the results of chanting the hymn. Apparently it will look like an exaggeration. But people have experienced miraculous results of obtaining the blessings of *Śrī Devī*. Only a dedicated mind is needed for the worship.

in the case of *Lalitā Triśatī* out of the 58.5 verses of this *phalashruti*, Lord *Hayagrīva* talks about and around this *Triśatī* and *Śrī Devī* for the first 27 verses and the results are mentioned only in the remaining verses.

हयग्रीव उवाच – *Hayagrīva uvāca* – Lord *Hayagrīva* said;

इत्येवं ते मयाख्यातं देव्या नामशतत्रयम् । रहस्यातिरहस्यद्वाद्गोपनीयं त्वया मुने ॥ १

Ityevam Te Mayākhyātam Devyā Nāmashtatrayam |
Rahasyātirahasyadvādgopanīyam Tvayā Mune II 1

Thus I instructed you Oh Sage! The three hundred names of *Śrī Devī*. This is a secret among secrets, hence O sage it has to be safely guarded.

शिववर्णाति नामानि श्रीदेव्या कथितानि हि । शत्तय्क्षराणि नामानि कामेशकथितानि च ॥ २

Śivavarnāti Nāmāni Śrīdevyā Kathitāni Hi |
Shattaykşarāni Nāmāni Kāmeśakathitāni Ca II 2

The names starting with *Śivākşarā*–s (male letters) were uttered by *Śrī Devī* and those names that begin with *Śaktiakşarā*–s (female letters) were uttered by Lord *Kāmeśa.*

उभयाक्षरनामानि ह्युभाभ्यांकथितानि वै । तदन्यैर्ग्रथितं स्तोत्रमेतस्य सदृशं किमु ॥ ३

Ubhayākshara nāmāni Hyubhābhyām Kathitāni Vai |
Tadanyairgrathitam Stotrametasya Sadrusham Kimu II 3

The names starting with *Ubhayakşāra*–s (*Hrīm* – neutral letter) are composed by them both. Hence, the works composed by others can ever be equal to this work? (*Ubhaya* means both – hence, *Ubhayakşarā*–s are those which represent the union of *Śiva–Śakti* or in other words, where *Śiva–Śakti* is represented or equally present together. This is known as *Śiva–Śakti Sāmarasyam.*

नानेन सदृशं स्तोत्रं श्रीदेवी प्रीतिदायकम् । लोकत्रयेऽपि कल्याणं सम्भवेन्नत्र संशय: ॥ ४

Nānena Sadruśam Stotram Śrī Devī Prītidāyakam |
LokatrayeSPi Kalyānam Sambhavennatra Samśayaḥ II 4

There is no work in all the three worlds that is equivalent to this most auspicious one, which gives joy to *Śrī Devī* and there is no doubt about it. *Sadrusha* means equivalent or similar – the idea here is there is no work that can be compared to this *Triśatī*. The reasons are twofold:

- Names starting with *Śiva, Shakti* and combined *aksharās,* which form her great mantra *Pancadaśākşarī* and
- The names are composed directly by *Śiva* couple themselves.

Jaganmāta is addressed here as *Śrī Devī*, even though this is a common epithet to *Mahālakshmī*, it is not specific to *Lakshmī* and here it denotes to *Śrīmātā*.

सूत उवाच - *Sūta Uvāca* – *Sūta* said;

इति हयमुखगीतं स्तोत्रराजं निशम्य प्रगलित कलुषोऽभूच्चित्तपर्याप्तिमेत्य।
निजगुरुमथ नत्वा कुम्भजन्मा तदुक्तं पुनरधिकरहस्यं ज्ञातुमेवं जगाद ॥ ५

Iti Hayamukhagītam Stotrarājam Niśamya Pragalita KalushoSBhūccittaparyāptimetya |
Nijagurumatha Natvā Kumbhajanmā Taduktam Punaradhikarahasyam Njātumevam Jagāda II 5

Hearing this sacred hymn from his *Guru*, sage Agastya's mind was hIghly satisfIed and wanted to get more knowledge about this secretive and dIvine *mantra*.

अगस्त्य उवाच - *Agastya Uvāca – Agastya* said;

अश्वानन महाभाग रहस्यमपि मे वद । शिववर्णानि कान्यत्र शक्तिवर्णानि कानि हि ॥ ६

Aśvānana Mahābhāga Rahasyamapi Me Vada |
Śivavarnāni Kānyatra Śaktivarnāni Kāni Hi II 6

उभयोरपि वर्णानि कनि वा वद देशिक । इति पृश्टः कुम्भजेन हयग्रीवोऽवदत्पुनः ॥ ७

Ubhayorapi Varnāni Kani Vā Vada Deshika |
Iti Pruşțaḥ Kumbhajena HayagrīvoऽVadatpunaḥ II 7

Oh! Lord *Hayagrīva* (***Ashvānana*** – horse faced), the lucky one, in what you have explained to me, help me to dIstinguIsh between the *Aksharas* (letters) of *Śiva* and *Shak*ti. What are the letters common to both of them? Even If It is a secret let me know. Hence, when Sage Agastya requested, the Lord started telling him the following lines.

हयग्रीव उवाच - *Hayagrīva Uvāca – Hayagrīva* said;

तव गोप्यं किमस्तीह साक्षादम्बानुशासनात् । इदं त्वतिरहस्यं ते वक्ष्यामि श्रृणु कुम्भज ॥ ८
Tava Gopyam Kimastīha Sākshādambānushāsanāt |
Idam Tvatirahasyam Te Vakşyāmi Śrunu Kumbhaja II 8

Oh! *Kumbha Munee* there is nothing to hIde from you. *Śrī Devī* herself appeared in person and ordained me to reveal It to you. I shall now reveal the ancIent secret to you.

एतद्विज्ञमात्रेण श्रीविद्या सिद्धिद भवेत् । कत्रयं हद्वयं चैव शैवो भागः प्रकीर्तितः ॥ ९

Etadvinjnamātrena Śrī Vidyā Siddhida Bhavet |
Katrayam Hadvayam Caiva Shaivo Bhāgaḥ Prakīrtitaḥ II 9

Out of the three hundred names, the inItial letters follow the order of *Pancadashī mantra*, which has the fIve masculine letters *Śiva–varnāni*, the three *Ka's* and the two *Ha's*, all the other remaining letters excepting *Hrīm* are the *Śaktyakşarās*, which are feminine letters. The letter *Hrīm*, which is the embodIment of both of them, was told by *Kāmeşvara* and *Kāmeşvarī*. The purpose of *Śrī Vidyā* will be fulfilled only after knowing the above difference.

शक्तक्षराणि शेषाणि ह्रीङ्कार उभयात्मक: । एवं विभागमज्ञात्वा ये विद्याजपशालिन: ॥ १०

Śaktakşarāni Śeshāni Hrīngkāra Ubhayātmakaḥ |
Evam Vibhāgamanjātvā Ye Vidyājapashālinaḥ II 10

Those who do not know this secret and the difference between the letters of *Śiva* and *Śakti* will not get the power even if recited crores of times.

न तेशां सिद्धिदा विद्या कल्पकोटिशतैरपि । चथुर्भि शिवचक्रैश्च शक्तिचक्रैश्च पञ्चभि: ॥ ११

Na Teśām Siddhidā Vidyā Kalpakoṭiśatairapi |
Cathurbhi Śivacakraiśca Śakticakraiśca Panjcabhiḥ II 11

The four *chakras* of *Śiva* and the five *chakras* of *Shak*ti become the nine *chakras*. The *Śrīchakra* is the body of *Śiva* and *Shakti*.

नव चक्रैश्च संसिद्धं श्रीचक्रं शिवयोर्वपु: । त्रिकोणमष्टकोणं च दशकोणद्वयं तथा ॥ १२

Nava Cakraiśca Samsiddham Śrīcakram Śivayorvapuḥ |
Trikoṇamaşṭakoṇam Ca Daśakoṇadvayam Tathā II 12

The circles of *Shakti* encapsulate the triangle, eight triangles, underlying ten triangles, outer ten triangles and the fourteen triangles. (Total – 43 triangles).

चतुर्दशारं चैतानि शक्तिचक्राणि पञ्च च । बिन्दुश्चाष्टदलंपद्मं पद्मं षोडशपत्रकम् ॥ १३

Caturdaśāram Caitāni Śakticakrāṇi Panjca Ca |
Binduścāşṭadalam Padmam Padmam Śoḍaśapatrakam II 13

The *Śiva chakra* embodies *Bindu*, the eight petalled lotus and the sixteen petalled lotus, including the squares.

चतुरश्रं च चत्वारि शिवचक्राण्यनुक्रमात् । त्रिकोणे बैन्दवं श्लिष्टं अष्टारेष्टदलाम्बुजम् ॥ १४

Caturaśram Ca Catvāri Śivacakrāṇyanukramāt |
Trikoṇe Baindavam Śliştam Aşṭāreşṭadalāmbujam II 14

Bindu is united with the triangle by encircling inside and the eight triangles are united with the eight petalled lotus. The two ten triangles are united with the sIxteen petalled lotus and the full–fledged square is unIted with the fourteen trIangles.

दशारयो: षोडशारं भूगृहं भुवनाश्रके। शैवानामपि शाक्तानां चक्राणां च परस्परं ॥ १५

Daśārayoḥ Śoḍashāram Bhūgruham Bhuvanāśrake |
Śaivānāmapi Śāktānām Cakrānām Ca Parasparam II 15

He who really knows the *Śrīchakra* will know the fact that the *Śiva chakra* and the *Shak*ti *chakra* are unIted forming the bond of *Abh*i*nnabhāva* (connection without break) relationshIp.

अविनाभाव सम्बन्धं यो जानाति स चक्रवित्। त्रिकोणरूपिणि शक्तिबिन्दुरूपपर: शिव: ॥ १६

Avinābhāva Sambandham Yo Jānāti Sa Cakravit |
Trikoṇarūpiṇi Śaktibindurūpaparaḥ Śivaḥ II 16

Kāmeśvarī Śakti is in the form of trIangle and Lord *Śiva* is in the form of *bindu*. The trIangle and the b*indu* are connected with *Abhinnabhāva* (connection without break) relationshIp.

अविनाभावसम्बन्धं तस्माद्बिन्दुत्रिकोणयो:। एवं विभागमज्ञात्वा श्रीचक्रं य: समर्चयेत् ॥ १७

Avinābhāvasambandham Tasmādbindutrikoṇayoḥ |
Evam Vibhāgamanjātvā Śrīcakram Yaḥ Samarcayet II 17

Those who do the *Śrīchakra* worshIp without knowing the *Abhinnabhāva* relationshIp will not be benefitted and also *Śrī Devī* will not be happy with his worshIp.

न तत्फलमवाप्नोति ललिताम्बा न तुष्यति। ये च जाननित् लोकेऽस्मिन्श्रीविद्याचक्रवेदिन: ॥ १८

Na Tatphalamavāpnoti Lalitāmbā Na Tushyati |
Ye Ca Jānanit LokeSSminśrī Vidyācakravedinaḥ II 18

Those who do not know about this relationshIp will not know about *Śrī Vidyā upāsana* and *Śrīchakra pooja* as well. Most of the people know about It generally but very few people know the intrIcate facts.

सामन्यवेदिन: सर्वे विशेषज्ञोऽतिदुर्लभ:। स्वयं विद्या विशेषज्ञो विशेषज्ञं समर्चयेत् ॥१९

Sāmanyavedinaḥ Sarve ViśeşanjoऽTidurlabhaḥ |
Svayam Vidyā Viśeşanjo Viśeşanjam Samarcayet II 19

Only a few people know about *Śrīchakra pooja* and *Śrī Vidyā Upāsana*. They should be worshIpped. Charity should be done to people who know about *Śrī Vidyā Upāsana* and *Śrīchakra pooja*. ReceIving something as charIty from *Śrī Vidyā Upāsakas* will also do utmost good.

तस्मै: देयं ततो ग्रह्यमशक्तस्तव्यदापयेत् । अन्धम्तमः प्रविशन्ति येऽव्द्यां समुपासते ॥ २०

Tasmaiḥ Deyam Tato Grahyamaśaktastavyadāpayet |
Andhamtamaḥ Pravishanti YeऽVdyām Samupāsate II 20

Those who follow the path of Ignorance are doomed into darkness. *Vedas* condemn people, who are not into *Śrī Vidyā upāsana* and encourages *Śrī Vidyā upāsakas*.

इति श्रुतिरपाहैतानविद्योपासकान्पुनः । विद्यान्योपासकानेव निन्दत्यारुणिकी श्रुतिः ॥ २१

Iti Śrutirapāhaitānavidyopāsakānpunaḥ |
Vidyānyopāsakāneva Nindatyāruṇikī Śrutiḥ II 21

अश्रुता सश्रुतासश्च यज्वानो येऽप्ययज्जवनः । स्वर्यन्तो नापेक्षन्ते इन्द्रमग्निञ्च ये विदुः ॥ २२

Aśrutā Saśrutāsashca Yajvāno YeऽPyayajjavanaḥ |
Svaryanto Nāpekşante indramagninjca Ye Viduḥ II 22

Śrī Vidyā pooja can be done by people who are educated and uneducated, those who perform the *yajnas* and also by those who do not. Those who worshIp indra and AgnI, other than Goddess *LalitāmbIkā* are consIdered worse than the particles of sand. They suffer in this lIfe and the lIfe after, says *ĀrunIkī Shruti*.

सिकता इव संयन्ति रश्मिभिः समुदीरिताः । अस्माल्लोकादमुष्माच्चेत्याह चानण्यक श्रुतिः ॥ २३

Sikatā Iva Samyanti Raśmibhiḥ Samudīritāḥ |
Asmāllokādamushmāccetyāha Cānaṇyaka Śrutiḥ II 23

Those who have no bIrth or who is an incarnation of *Śiva* are inItiated into the *Pancadaśākşarī mantra*.

यस्य नो पश्चिमं जन्म यदि वाश्ङ्करः स्वयम् । तेनैव लभ्यते विद्या श्रीमत्पञ्चदशाक्षरी ॥ २४

Yasya No Paścimam Janma Yadi Vāshngkaraḥ Svayam |
Tenaiva Labhyate Vidyā Śrīmatpancadaśākṣarī II 24

in *tantra* and *mantra shāstras* the greatness of *Śrī Vidyā* is eulogIzed. *Śrī Vidyā* is the only way to attain *moksha*. There is no doubt in this.

इति मन्त्रेषु बहुधा विद्याया महिमोच्यते । मोक्षैकहेतुविद्या तु श्रीविद्या नात्र संशयः ॥ २५

Iti Mantreṣu Bahudhā Vidyāyā Mahimocyate |
Mokṣaikahetuvidyā Tu Śrī Vidyā Nātra Samśayaḥ II 25

न शिल्पदि ज्ञानयुक्ते विद्वच्छब्धः प्रयुज्यते । मोक्षैकहेतुविद्या सा श्रीविद्यैव न संशयः ॥ २६

Na Śilpadi Njānayukte Vidvacchabdhaḥ Prayujyate |
Mokṣaikahetuvidyā Sā Śrīvidyaiva Na Samshayaḥ II 26

The people who are proficIent in muslc and sculpture are not consldered as real vIdwans (scholars). Hence, in this context *Śrī Vidyā upāsaka* is the real vIdwan. Therefore, the wIse people should gIve charIty to *Śrī Vidyā upāsakas* and propagate the great values of *Śrī Vidyā*.

तस्माद्विद्यादेवात्र विद्वान्विद्वानितीर्यते । स्वयं विद्याविदे दद्यात्ख्यापयेत्तद्गु णान्सुधी ॥ २७

Tasmādvidyādevātra Vidvānvidvānitīryate |
Svayam Vidyāvide Dadyātkhyāpayettadguṇānsudhīḥ II 27

स्वयंविद्यारहस्यज्ञो विद्यामाहात्म्यमवेद्यपि । विद्याविदं नार्चयेच्चेत्को वा तं पूजतेज्जनः ॥ २८

Svayamvidyārahasyanjo Vidyāmāhātmyamavedyapi |
Vidyāvidam Nārcayeccetko Vā Tam Pūjatejjanaḥ II 28

If the devotees knowing the greatness of this *Vidyā*, do not respect the true *Śrī Vidyā upāsakas*, then who will respect? *Hayagrīva* told Agastya that he was supposed to tell him something but It was leading to another and that he would tell the facts that he was instructed to tell him.

प्रसङ्गादिदमुक्तं ते प्रकृतं श्रृणु कुम्भज । यः कीर्तयेत्सकृत्भक्त्या दिव्यनामशतत्रयम् ॥ २९

Prasanggādidamuktam Te Prakrutam Śruṇu Kumbhaja |
Yaḥ Kīrtayetsakrutbhaktyā Divyanāmaśatatrayam II 29

Now I shall tell you the beneflts of these three hundred holy names when recited even once with reverence.

तस्य पुण्यमहं वक्ष्ये श्रृणु त्वं कुम्भसंभव। रहस्यनामसाहरपाठे यत्फलमीरितम् ॥ ३०

Tasya Puṇyamaham Vakṣye Śruṇu Tvam Kumbhasambhava |
Rahasyanāmasāharapāṭhe Yatphalamīritam ll 30

The recitation of a single name of this *Triśatī* is more effective and powerful than the recitation of the *sahasranāma* crores of times.

तत्फलं कोटिकुणितमेकनामजपाद्भवेत्। कामेश्वरीकामेशाभ्यां कृतं नामशतत्रयम् ॥ ३१

Tatphalam Koṭikuṇitamekanāmajapādbhavet |
Kāmeśvarīkāmeśābhyām Krutam Nāmaśatatrayam ll 31

This sacred *Triśatī* hymn is recited by *Kāmeśvarī* and *Kameśvara* and it can never be equal to any other hymn composed by others.

नान्येन तुलयेदेतत्स्तोत्रेणान्य कृतेन च। श्रियः परम्परा यस्य भावि वा चोत्तरोत्तरम् ॥ ३२

Nānyena Tulayedetatstotreṇānya Krutena Ca |
Shriyaḥ Paramparā Yasya Bhāvi Vā Cottarottaram ll 32

Those who recite this *Triśatī*, he and his families would attain prosperity not only in this generation but in future generations also.

तेनैव लभ्यते चैतत्पश्चाच्छ्रेयः परीक्षयेत्। अस्या नाम्नां त्रिशत्यास्तु महिमा केन वर्णयते ॥ ३३

Tenaiva Labhyate Caitatpaścācchreyaḥ Parīkṣayet |
Asyā Nāmnām Triśatyāstu Mahimā Kena Varṇayate ll 33

Who can describe the efficacy of the holy and sacred *stotra* coming out from the lotus mouth of the divine couple?

या स्वयं शिवयोर्वक्त्रपद्माभ्यां परिनिःसृता। नित्यं षोडशसङ्ख्याकान्विप्रानादौ तु भोजयेत् ॥ ३४

Yā Svayam Śivayorvaktrapadmābhyām Pariniḥsrutā |
Nityam Śoḍaśasangkhyākānviprānādou Tu Bhojayet ll 34

Sixteen *Śrī Vidyā upāsakas* should be considered as the sixteen *Nityā devīs* and should be anointed with perfumed oil with fragrant herbal, powder and given head bath with hot water.

अभ्यक्ताम्स्तिलतैलेन स्नातानुष्णेन वारिणा। अब्यच्र्य गन्धपुष्पाद्यैः कामेश्वर्यादिनामभिः ॥ ३५

Abhyaktāmstilatailena Snātānushṇena Vāriṇā |
Abyarcya Gandhapuşpādyaiḥ Kāmeśvaryādināmabhiḥ II 35

सूपापूपैः शर्कराद्यैः पायसैः फलसंयुतैः । विद्याविदो विशेषेण भोजयेत्षोडश द्विजान् ॥ ३६

Sūpāpūpaiḥ Sharkarādyaiḥ Pāyasaiḥ Phalasamyutaiḥ |
Vidyāvido Viśeşeṇa Bhojayetşoḍaśa Dvijān II 36

Anoint the sixteen *nityā devīs* including the *mahānityā Kāmeśvarī* with sandal paste and adorn them with fine clothing. Then invite the *nityā devīs* and perform *Archana* to them, offering *appam*, sugar, ghee and fruits. Offer them the food having all the six tastes.

एवं नित्यार्चनं कुर्यातादौ ब्रह्मण भोजनम् । त्रिशतीनामभिः पर्चाद्ब्राह्मणान्क्रमशोऽर्चयेत् ॥ ३७

Evam Nityārcanam Kuryātādou Brāhmaṇa Bhojanam |

Triśatīnāmabhiḥ ParcādbrāhmaṇānkramashoSRcayet II 37

Archana should be done on these brahmins with 300 names of this *Triśatī* and then food should be offered as done to *Śrī Devī* during *pooja*.

तैलाभ्यङ्गातिकं दत्वा विभते सति भक्तितः । शुक्लप्रतिपदारभ्य पौर्णमास्यवधि क्रमात् ॥ ३८

Tailābhyanggātikam Datvā Vibhate Sati Bhaktitaḥ |
Śuklapratipadārabhya Pourṇamāsyavadhi Kramāt II 38

Such a *pooja* should be done on Brahmins during the first day of *shukla paksha* (bright lunar fortnight) or on a full Moon day – they should be worshipped with devotion by offering oil to take bath, new dress, etc.

दिवसे दिवसे विप्रा भोज्या विम्शतीसङ्ख्यया । दशभिः पञ्चभिर्वापि त्रीभिरेकनवा दिनैः ॥ ३९

Divase Divase Viprā Bhojyā Vimśatīsangkhyayā |
Dashabhiḥ Panjcabhirvāpi Trībhirekanavā Dinaiḥ II 39

Such a worship can be done for 20 days continuously on a daily basis. This can also be done on a single day – on the 10th day or 5th day of bright Lunar fortnight.
त्रिम्शत्षष्टिः शतं विप्राः सम्भोज्यस्त्रिशतं क्रमात् । एवं यः कुरुते भक्त्या जन्ममध्ये सकृन्नरः ॥ ४०

Trimshatshaşṭiḥ Shatam Viprāḥ Sambhojyastrishatam Kramāt |
Evam Yaḥ Kurute Bhaktyā Janmamadhye Sakrunnaraḥ II 40

The person chanting this *Triśatī* with devotion and feeding the 300 Brahmins will lIve long lIfe and will not have further bIrth.

तस्यैव सफलं जन्म मुक्तिस्तस्य करे स्थिरा: । रहस्यनामसाहस्रभोजनेऽप्येवमेव हि ॥ ४१

Tasyaiva Saphalam Janma Muktistasya Kare Sthirāḥ |
RahasyanāmasāhasrabhojaneSPyevamevahi II 41

The devotees who feed 1000 brahmins and do worshIp of this secret *Triśatī* will attain the *moksha* ImmedIately.

आदौ नित्यबलिं कुर्यात्पश्चाद्ब्राह्मणभोजनम् । रहस्यनामसाहरमहिमा यो मयोदित: ॥ ४२

Ādou Nityabalim Kuryātpaścād Brāhmaṇa Bhojanam |
Rahasyanāma Sāharamahimā Yo Mayoditaḥ II 42

SIxteen Brahmins have to be chosen and offered water, cleaning of feet, seat, oIl bath in hot water, etc. The 16 titi *nItyā Devīs* and *Mahānityā devī* have to be Imagined on these 16 Brahmins. WorshIpping them with 16 offerings has to be completed. All the 16 *Devīs* have to be worshIpped lIke *HrīmŚrīm Kāmeshwaryai Namaḥ, HrīmŚrīm BagamālinyaI Namaḥ* and so on. *Tarpaṇa* has to be done by them. These 16 Brahmins are made to sIt facing East or North. They have to be offered clothes, sandal paste, jewels, flowers, other fragrant materIals, fragrant smoke, lIght, etc. Then they have to be fed with sweet, fruIts, etc. They have to be bowed after gIven betel leaves and money (*dakshiṇa*). Such worshIp is called *Nitya Bali*. This has to be followed with feeding of 300 Brahmins. If It could be done on a single day that would be great, else, It could be for 15 days at the rate of 20 per day. Thus the count of 300 has to be completed – this is also a great accomplIshment. That too It can be from the fIrst day of the brIght lunar fortnIght till the full Moon day – the Brahmins have to be Imagined with the 300 names in *Triśatī*. All these days the worshIpper has to follow the vow oblIgations. The *NItya BalI* worshIp has to be done on the starting day.

सशिकराणुरत्रैकनाम्नो महिमवारिधे: । वाग्देवीरचिते नामसाहस्रे यद्यदीरितम् ॥ ४३

Saśikarāṇuratraikanāmno Mahimavāridheḥ |
Vāgdevīracite Nāmasāhasre Yadyadīritam II 43

These 300 names are more powerful than the 1000 names uttered by the same *Vāgdevīs*.

तत्फलं कोटिगुणितं नाम्नोऽप्येकस्य कीर्तनात् । एतन्यैर्जपै: स्तोत्रैरर्चनैर्यत्फलं भवेत् ॥ ४४

Tatphalam Koṭiguṇitam NāmnoSPyekasya Kīrtanāt |
Etanyairjapaiḥ Stotrairarcanairyatphalam Bhavet II 44

The result will multiply crores of times respectively, If these 300 names are Sung, or chant as a hymn or done as a *japa* of indIvIdual names or done as *Archana.*

तत्फलं कोटिगुणितं भवेन्नामशतत्रयात् । वाग्देविरचितास्तोत्रे तादृशो महिमा यदि ॥ ४५

Tatphalam Koṭiguṇitam Bhavennāmashatatrayāt |
Vāgdeviracitāstotre Tādrusho Mahimā Yadi II 45

If this hymn is chant after worshIpping the *vāgdevīs*, the result will multiply crores of times.

साक्षात्कामेशकामेशी कृतेऽस्मिन्गृह्यतामिति । स्कृत्सङ्कीर्तनादेव नाम्नाम्नस्मिञ्शतत्रये ॥ ४६

Sākşātkāmeśakāmeśī KruteSSmingruhytāmiti |
Skrutsangkīrtanādeva Nāmnāmnasminjśatatraye II 46

This *Triśatī* hymn was uttered by the divine couple. Hence If this is Sung in any house, *Devas* will resIde in that house.

भवेच्चित्तस्य पर्याप्तिन्यूर्नमन्यानपेक्षिणी । न ज्ञातव्यमितोऽप्यन्यत्र जप्तव्यञ्च कुम्भज ॥ ४७

Bhaveccittasya Paryaptinyūrnamanyānapekshiṇī |
Na NjātavyamitoSPyanyatra Japtavyanjca Kumbhaja II 47

Oh *Kumbha munee*! The devotee, who chants this hymn, will defInItely get whatever he asks.

सद्यत्साध्यतमं कार्यं तत्तदर्थमिदञ्जपेत् । तत्तत्फलमवाप्नोति पश्चात्कार्यं परीक्षयेत् ॥ ४८

Sadyatsādhyatamam Kāryam Tattadarthamidanjjapet | Tattatphalamavāpnoti Paścātkāryam Parīkşayet II 48

If this hymn is genuinely chant with any particular objective or purpose that objective or purpose will defInItely be met by *Śrī Devī* to her devotee. Once the devotion is Important.

ये ये प्रयोगास्तन्त्रेषु तैस्तैर्यत्साध्यते फलं । तत्सर्वं सिद्ध्यति क्षिप्रं नामत्रिशतकीर्तनात् ॥ ४९

Ye Ye Prayogāstantreşu Taistairyatsādhyate Phalam |
Tatsarvam Siddhyati Kşipram Nāmatrishatakīrtanāt II 49

If any particular results are sought for, If devotee does *pooja*, after understanding and following the process of chanting this *Triśatī*, all those results will be bestowed on that devotee.

आयुष्करं पुष्टिकरं पुत्रदं वश्यकारकम् । विद्याप्रदं कीर्तिकरं सुखवित्वप्रदायकम् ॥ ५०

Āyuşkaram Puşţikaram Putradam Vaśyakārakam |
Vidyāpradam Kīrtikaram Sukhavitvapradāyakam II 50

This *Triśatī* will definltely provlde long llfe, well nourishment, children, attractiveness, knowledge through education, fame and pleasant life.

सर्वसम्पत्प्रदं सर्वभोगदं सर्वसौख्यदम् । सर्वाभिष्टप्रदं चैव देव्या नामशतत्रयम् ॥ ५१

Sarvasampatpradam Sarvabhogadam Sarvasoukhyadam |
Sarvābhişţapradam Caiva Devyā Nāmaśatatrayam II 51

This *Triśatī* will definltely provlde all wealth, every kind of enjoyment, safe life and meeting of all wishes.

एतज्जपपरो भूयान्नान्यदिच्छेत्कदाचन। एतत्कीर्तनसन्तुष्टा श्रीदेवी ललिताम्बिका ॥ ५२

Etajjapaparo Bhūyānnānyadicchetkadācana |
Etatkīrtanasantuşţā Śrī Devī Lalitāmbikā II 52

Japa of this hymn has to be made with focused mind on *Śrī Devī Lalitā* without any other type of thinking.

The words of Lord Krishna in *Śrīmad Bhagavad Gīta* (9–22) is vltal and can be reminded at this juncture, even at the cost of duplication:

Ananyāśchintayanto Mām Te Janāḥ Paryupāsate |
Teshām Nithyābhi Yuktānām Yogakşemam Vahāmaham II

भक्तस्य यद्यदिष्टं स्यात्तत्तत्पूरयते धृवं । तस्मात्कुंभोद्भवमुने कीर्तय त्वमिदम् सदा ॥ ५३

Bhaktasya Yadyadişţam Syāttattatpūrayate Dhruvam |
Tasmātkumbhodbhavamune Kīrtaya Tvamidam Sadā II 53

Oh *Kumbha* munee! The devotee who always sings this *Triśatī* will get all his wishes definltely satiated.

नापरं किञ्चिदपि ते बोद्धव्यं नावशिष्यते । इति ते कथितं स्तोत्रं ललिता प्रीतिदायकम् ॥ ५४

Nāparam Kinjcidapi Te Boddhavyam Nāvashishyate |
Iti Te Kathitam Stotram Lalitā Prītidāyakam II 54

The devotee who reads or hears this *stora*, which is so affectionate to *Lalitādevī,* need not go to any other *devas* for any purpose. (It is imperative that *Śrī Devī* herself will provide all the needs).

नाविद्यावेदिने ब्रूयान्नाभक्ताय कदाचन । न शठाय न दु ष्टाय नाविश्वासाय कर्हिचित् ॥ ५५

Nāvidyāvedine Brūyānnābhaktāya Kadācana |
Na Śaṭhāya Na Duṣṭāya Nāviśvāsāya Karhicit II 55

The chanter or hearer of this hymn can be;

- Not a hlghly knowledgeable person
- Not be a great devotee
- Have not seen *Śrī Devī*
- Not even have conf Idence on **her**.

यो ब्रूयात्रिशतीं नाम्नां तस्यानर्थो महान्भवेत् । इत्याज्ञा शाङ्करी प्रोक्ता तस्माद्गोप्यमिदं त्वया ॥ ५६

Yo Brūyātriśatīm Nāmnām Tasyānartho Mahānbhavet |
Ityānjā Shāngkarī Proktā Tasmādgopyamidam Tvayā II 56

The meaning of these 300 names told by *Shankarī* herself has to be understood and chant, then the devotee will become a great *upāsaka*.

ललिता प्रेरितेनैव मयोक्तम् स्तोत्रमुत्तमम् । रहस्यनामसाहस्रादपि गोप्यमिदं मुने ॥ ५७

Lalitā Preritenaiva Mayoktam Stotramuttamam |
Rahasyanāmasāhasrādapi Gopyamidam Mune II 57

Oh sage! The hlghest and secretive *stotra*, which is so fond to *Lalitādevī* has been uttered by me to you. This is more secret than *Lalitā Sahasranāma.*

सूत उवाच - *Sūta Uvāca* – *Sūta* said;

एवमुक्त्वा हयग्रीव: कुम्भजं तापसोत्तमम् । स्तोत्रेणानेन ललितां स्तुत्वा त्रिपुरसुन्दरी ॥ ५८
आनन्दलहरीमग्नमानस: समवर्तत ॥

Evamuktvā Hayagrīvaḥ Kumbhajam Tāpasottamam |
Stotreṇānena Lalitām Stutvā Tripurasundarī ll 58
Ānandalaharīmagnamānasaḥ Samavartata ll

Thus sage Agastya, advised by Lord *Hayagrīva* started worshipping *Śrī Lalitā Devī Tripura Sundarī* with bliss and happiness.

The gist of this *phalashruti* is;

Chanting *Lalitā Triśatī* even once sets the mind–set straight and clean. The more one chants or even hears, the more one takes steps forward. Lord *Hayagrīva* assured sage Agastya that by chanting *Lalitā Triśatī* even once would help to attain peace of mind. Its practice without desires transforms the heart, mind and soul. Fulfillment follows as a consequence, for the decider is *Lalitā* **Herself**. As one sows, so one reaps!

Hayagrīva also told Agastya that out of the 15 letters of *Pancadashaksharī Mantra* the letters *Ka* (thrice repeated) and *Ha* (twice repeated) are the letters indicating *Śiva*, *Hrīm* (thrice repeated) is a letter indicating *Śiva* and *Shak*ti as well as the *Trimūr*tis and the rest of the seven letters are the letters indicating *Shak*ti. Then *Hayagrīva* explains to Agastya the formation of *Śrīchakra*. He also tells him that:

- Just by one repetition of the *Lalitā Triśatī stotra*, the mind becomes full of contentment and peace.
- All that can be attained by *Tantra shāstras* can be attained by chanting of this great *stotra*.
- Without any desire, if a devotee chants these, *Śrī Devī* would judge what he wants and give him all those.
- People without devotion and honesty should never chant this because they may have to face the consequences of negative effects.

इति श्री ब्रमाण्ड पुराणे उत्तरखाण्डे श्री हयग्रीवागस्त्यसंवादे
श्रीललितात्रिशती स्तोत्र कथनं संपूर्णम्

Iti Śrī Bramāṇḍa Purāṇe Uttarakhāṇḍe Śrī Hayagrīvāgastya Samvāde Śrī Lalitā Triśatī Stotra Kathanam Sampūrnam

Thus ends the *Śrī Lalitā Triśatī* hymn, forming part of *Uttara Khāṇḍa* of *Brahmāṇḍa Puraṇa*, as a dialogue between *Śrī Hayagrīva* and Agastya.

Oṃ Tat Sat

*****

Annexure 1

300 names chronologically;

Śrīmadvāgbhavakūṭam – श्रीमद्वाग्भवकूटम्		
	Ka	क
1.	Kakārarūpā	ककाररूपा
2.	Kalyāṇī	कल्याणी
3.	Kalyāṇa Guṇaśālinī	कल्याण गुणशालिनी
4.	Kalyāṇa Śailanilayā	कल्याण शैलनिलया
5.	Kamanīyā	कमनीया
6.	Kalāvatī	कलावती
7.	Kamalākṣī	कमलाक्षी
8.	Kalmaṣaghnī	कल्मषघ्नी
9.	Karuṇāmruta Sāgarā	करुणामृत सागरा
10.	Kadambakānana Vāsā	कदम्बकानन वासा
11.	Kadamba Kusumapriyā	कदम्ब कुसुमप्रिया
12.	Kandarpa Vidhyā	कन्दर्प विध्या
13.	Kandarpa Janakāpāṅga Vīkṣaṇā	कन्दर्प जनकापाङ्ग वीक्षणा
14.	Karpūravīṭi Sourabhya Kallolita Kakuptaṭā	कर्पूरवीटि सौरभ्य कल्लोलित ककुप्तटा
15.	Kalidoṣaharā	कलिदोषहरा
16.	Kañjalocanā	कञ्जलोचना
17.	Kamravigrahā	कम्रविग्रहा
18.	Karmādi Sākṣiṇī	कर्मादि साक्षिणी
19.	Kārayitrī	कारयित्री
20.	Karmaphalapradā	कर्मफलप्रदा
	E	ए
21.	Ekāra Rūpā	एकार रूपा
22.	Ekākṣarī	एकाक्षरी
23.	Ekānekākṣarākrutiḥ	एकानेकाक्षराकृति:

24.	*Etattaditya Nirdeśyā*	एतत्तदित्य निर्देश्या
25.	*Ekānanda Cidākrutiḥ*	एकानन्द चिदाकृति:
26.	*Evamityāgamābodhyā*	एवमित्यागमाबोध्या
27.	*Ekabhaktimadarcitā*	एकभक्तिमदर्चिता
28.	*Ekāgracitta Nirdhyātā*	एकाग्रचित्त निर्ध्याता
29.	*Eṣaṇā Rahitāddhrutā*	एषणा रहिताद्धृता
30.	*Elāsugamdhi Cikurā*	एलासुगंधि चिकुरा
31.	*Enaḥ Kūṭa Vināśinī*	एन:कूट विनाशिनी
32.	*Ekabhogā*	एकभोगा
33.	*Ekarasā*	एकरसा
34.	*Ekaiśvarya Pradāyinī*	एकैश्वर्य प्रदायिनी
35.	*Ekātapatra Sāmrājyapradā*	एकातपत्र साम्राज्यप्रदा
36.	*Ekānta Pūjitā*	एकान्त पूजिता
37.	*Edhamānaprabhā*	एधमानप्रभा
38.	*Ejadanejajjagadīśvarī*	एजदनेजज्जगदीश्वरी
39.	*Ekavīrādi Samsevyā*	एकवीरादि संसेव्या
40.	*Ekaprābhava Śālinī*	एकप्राभव शालिनी
	Ee	ई
41.	*Eekārarūpā*	ईकाररूपा
42.	*Eeśitrī*	ईशित्री
43.	*Eepsitārtha Pradāyinī*	ईप्सितार्थ प्रदायिनी
44.	*Eeddrugityavinirdeśyā*	ईद्दृगित्यविनिर्देश्या
45.	*Eeśvaratva Vidhāyinī*	ईश्वरत्व विधायिनी
46.	*Eeśānādibrahmamayī*	ईशानादिब्रह्ममयी
47.	*Eeśitvādyaṣṭasiddhidā*	ईशित्वाद्यष्टसिद्धिदा
48.	*Eekṣitrī*	ईक्षित्री
49.	*Eekṣaṇasruṣṭāṇḍakoṭiḥ*	ईक्षणसृष्टाण्डकोटि:
50.	*Eeśvaravallabhā*	ईश्वरवल्लभा

51.	*Eeḍitā*	ईडिता
52.	*Eeśvarārdhāṅgaśarīrā*	ईश्वरार्धाङ्गशरीरा
53.	*Eeśādhidevatā*	ईशाधिदेवता
54.	*Eeśvarapreraṇakarī*	ईश्वरप्रेरणकरी
55.	*Eeśatāṇḍavasākṣiṇī*	ईशताण्डवसाक्षिणी
56.	*Eeśvarotsaṅganilayā*	ईश्वरोत्सङ्गनिलया
57.	*Eetibādhāvināśinī*	ईतिबाधाविनाशिनी
58.	*Eehāvirāhitā*	ईहाविराहिता
59.	*Eeśaśakti*	ईशशक्ति
60.	*Eeṣatsmitānanā*	ईषत्स्मितानना
	La	ल
61.	*Lakārarūpā*	लकाररूपा
62.	*Lalitā*	ललिता
63.	*Lakṣmīvāṇī Niṣevitā*	लक्ष्मीवाणी निषेविता
64.	*Lākinī*	लाकिनी
65.	*Lalanārūpā*	ललनारूपा
66.	*Lasaddhāḍimapāṭalā*	लसद्धाडिमपाटला
67.	*Lalantikā Lasatphālā*	ललन्तिका लसत्फाला
68.	*Lalāṭanayanārcitā*	ललाटनयनार्चिता
69.	*Lakṣanojjvala Divyāṅgī*	लक्षनोज्ज्वल दिव्याङ्गी
70.	*Lakṣakoṭyaṇḍa Nāyikā*	लक्षकोट्यण्ड नायिका
71.	*Lakṣyārthā*	लक्ष्यार्था
72.	*Lakṣṇāgamyā*	लक्ष्णागम्या
73.	*Labdhakāmā*	लब्धकामा
74.	*Latātanuḥ*	लतातनु:
75.	*Lalāmarājadalikā*	ललामराजदलिका
76.	*Lambimuktālatāṅcitā*	लम्बिमुक्तालताञ्चिता
77.	*Lambodaraprasūḥ*	लम्बोदरप्रसू:
78.	*Labhyā*	लभ्या

79.	*Lajjāḍhyā*	लज्जाढ्या
80.	*Layavarjitā*	लयवर्जिता
	Hrīm	ह्रीं
81.	*Hrīmkāra Rūpā*	ह्रींकार रूपा
82.	*Hrīmkāra Nilayā*	ह्रींकार निलया
83.	*Hrīmpadapriyā*	ह्रींपदप्रिया
84.	*Hrīmkāra Bījā*	ह्रींकार बीजा
85.	*Hrīmkāra Mantrā*	ह्रींकार मन्त्रा
86.	*Hrīmkāra Lakṣaṇā*	ह्रींकार लक्षणा
87.	*Hrīmkāra Japasuprītā*	ह्रींकार जपसुप्रीता
88.	*Hrīmmatiḥ*	ह्रींमति:
89.	*Hrīm Vibhūṣaṇā*	ह्रीं विभूषणा
90.	*Hrīm Śīlā*	ह्रीं शीला
91.	*Hrīmpadārādhyā*	ह्रींपदाराध्या
92.	*Hrīm Garbhā*	ह्रीं गर्भा
93.	*Hrīmpadābhidhā*	ह्रींपदाभिधा
94.	*Hrīmkāra Vācyā*	ह्रींकार वाच्या
95.	*Hrīmkāra Pūjyā*	ह्रींकार पूज्या
96.	*Hrīmkāra Pīṭhikā*	ह्रींकार पीठिका
97.	*Hrīmkāra Vedyā*	ह्रींकार वेद्या
98.	*Hrīmkāra Cintyā*	ह्रींकार चिन्त्या
99.	*Hrīm*	ह्रीं
100.	*Hrīm Śarīriṇī*	ह्रीं शरीरेणी
Madhyakūṭam – मध्यकूटम्		
	Ha	ह
101.	*Hakārarūpā*	हकाररूपा
102.	*Haladhrutpūjitā*	हलधृत्पूजिता
103.	*Hariṇekṣṇā*	हरिणेक्ष्णा

104.	*Haripriyā*	हरिप्रिया
105.	*Harārādhyā*	हराराध्या
106.	*Haribrahmendra Vanditā*	हरिब्रह्मेन्द्र वन्दिता
107.	*Hayārūḍhāsevitāmghriḥ*	हयारूढासेवितांघ्रिः
108.	*Hayamedhasamarcitā*	हयमेधसमर्चिता
109.	*Haryakṣavāhanā*	हर्यक्षवाहना
110.	*Hamsavāhanā*	हंसवाहना
111.	*Hatadānavā*	हतदानवा
112.	*Hatyādi Pāpaśamanī*	हत्यादि पापशमनी
113.	*Haridaśvādi Sevitā*	हरिदश्वादि सेविता
114.	*Hastikumbhottuṅkakucā*	हस्तिकुम्भोत्तुङ्ककुचा
115.	*Hastikruttipriyāṅganā*	हस्तिकृत्तिप्रियाङ्गना
116.	*Haridrākuṅkumādigdhā*	हरिद्राकुङ्कुमादिग्धा
117.	*Haryaśvādyamarārcitā*	हर्यश्वाद्यमरार्चिता
118.	*Harkeśasakhī*	हर्केशसखी
119.	*Hādividyā*	हादिविद्या
120.	*Hālāmadālasā*	हालामदालसा
	Sa	स
121.	*Sakārarūpā*	सकाररूपा
122.	*Sarvaṅā*	सर्वज्ञा
123.	*Sarveśī*	सर्वेशी
124.	*Sarvamaṅgalā*	सर्वमङ्गला
125.	*Sarvakartrī*	सर्वकर्त्री
126.	*Sarvabhartrī*	सर्वभर्त्री
127.	*Sarvahantrī*	सर्वहन्त्री
128.	*Sanātanā*	सनातना
129.	*Sarvanavadyā*	सर्वनवद्या
130.	*Sarvāṅga Sundarī*	सर्वाङ्ग सुन्दरी
131.	*Sarvasākṣiṇī*	सर्वसाक्षिणी

132.	*Sarvātmikā*	सर्वात्मिका
133.	*Sarvasoukhyadātrī*	सर्वसौख्यदात्री
134.	*Sarva Vimohinī*	सर्व विमोहिनी
135.	*Sarvādhārā*	सर्वाधारा
136.	*Sarvagatā*	सर्वगता
137.	*Sarvāvaguṇavarjitā*	सर्वावगुणवर्जिता
138.	*Sarvāruṇā*	सर्वारुणा
139.	*Sarvamātā*	सर्वमाता
140.	*Sarvabhūṣaṇabhūṣitā*	सर्वभूषणभूषिता
	Ka	क
141.	*Kakārārthā*	ककारार्था
142.	*Kālahantrī*	कालहन्त्री
143.	*Kāmeśī*	कामेशी
144.	*Kāmitārthadā*	कामितार्थदा
145.	*Kāmasaṅjīvinī*	कामसञ्जीविनी
146.	*Kalyā*	कल्या
147.	*Kaṭhinastana Maṇḍalā*	कठिनस्तन मण्डला
148.	*Karabhoruḥ*	करभोरु:
149.	*Kalānāthamukhī*	कलानाथमुखी
150.	*Kacajitāmbhudā*	कचजिताम्भुदा
151.	*Kaṭākṣasyandi Karuṇā*	कटाक्षस्यन्दि करुणा
152.	*Kapāliprāṇanāyikā*	कपालिप्राणनायिका
153.	*Kāruṇyavigrahā*	कारुण्यविग्रहा
154.	*Kāntā*	कान्ता
155.	*Kāntidhūtajapāvaliḥ*	कान्तिधूतजपावलि:
156.	*Kalālāpā*	कलालापा
157.	*Kambukaṇṭhī*	कम्बुकण्ठी
158.	*Karanirjitapallavā*	करनिर्जितपल्लवा

159.	*Kalpavallīsamabhujā*	कल्पवल्लीसमभुजा
160.	*Kastūritilakāṅcitā*	कस्तूरितिलकाञ्चिता
	Ha	ह
161.	*Hakārārthā*	हकारार्था
162.	*Hamsa Gatiḥ*	हंस गतिः
163.	*Hāṭakābharaṇojvalā*	हाटकाभरणोज्वला
164.	*Hāraharikucābhogā*	हारहरिकुचाभोगा
165.	*Hākinī*	हाकिनी
166.	*Halyavarjitā*	हल्यवर्जिता
167.	*Haritpati Samārādhyā*	हरित्पति समाराध्या
168.	*Haṭhātkāra Hatāsurā*	हठात्कार हतासुरा
169.	*Harṣapradā*	हर्षप्रदा
170.	*Havirbhoktrī*	हविर्भोक्त्री
171.	*Hārda Santamasāpahā*	हार्द सन्तमसापहा
172.	*Hallīsalāsya Santuṣṭā*	हल्लीसलास्य सन्तुष्टा
173.	*Hamsa Mantrārthā Rūpiṇī*	हंस मन्त्रार्था रूपिणी
174.	*Hānopādāna Nirmuktā*	हानोपादान निर्मुक्ता
175.	*Harṣiṇī*	हर्षिणी
176.	*Hari Sodarī*	हरि सोदरी
177.	*Hāhā Hūhū Mukhastutyā*	हाहा हूहू मुखस्तुत्या
178.	*Hāni Vruddhi Vivarjitā*	हानि वृद्धि विवर्जिता
179.	*Hayyaṅgavīna Hrudayā*	हय्यङ्गवीन हृदया
180.	*Harigopāruṇāmśukā*	हरिगोपारुणांशुका
	La	ल
181.	*Lakārākhyā*	लकाराख्या
182.	*Latāpūjyā*	लतापूज्या
183.	*Layasthiti Udbhaveśvarī*	लयस्थिति उद्भवेश्वरी
184.	*Lāsya Darśana Santuṣṭā*	लास्य दर्शन सन्तुष्टा
185.	*Lābhālābhā Vivarjitā*	लाभालाभा विवर्जिता

186.	*Laṅghyetarāṅā*	लङ्घ्येतराज्ञा
187.	*Lāvaṇya Śālinī*	लावण्य शालिनी
188.	*Laghusiddhidā*	लघुसिद्धिदा
189.	*Lākṣārasasavarṇābhā*	लाक्षारससवर्णाभा
190.	*Lakṣmaṇāgraja Pūjitā*	लक्ष्मणाग्रज पूजिता
191.	*Labhyetarā*	लभ्येतरा
192.	*Labdha Bhakti Sulabhā*	लब्ध भक्ति सुलभा
193.	*Lāṅgalāyudhā*	लाङ्गलायुधा
194.	*Lagnacāmara Hasta Śrī Śāradā Parivījitā*	लग्नचामर हस्त श्री शारदा परिवीजिता
195.	*Lajjāpada Samārādhyā*	लज्जापद समाराध्या
196.	*Lampaṭā*	लंपटा
197.	*Lakuleśvarī*	लकुलेश्वरी
198.	*Labdhamānā*	लब्धमाना
199.	*Labdharasā*	लब्धरसा
200.	*Labdha Sampat Samunnatiḥ*	लब्ध संपत् समुन्नतिः
	Hrīm	ह्रीं
201.	*Hrīmkāriṇī*	ह्रींकारिणी
202.	*Hrīmkārādiḥ*	ह्रींकारादिः
203.	*Hrīmmadhyā*	ह्रींमध्या
204.	*Hrīmśikhāmaṇiḥ*	ह्रींशिखामणिः
205.	*Hrīmkāra Kuṇḍāgni Śikhā*	ह्रींकार कुण्डाग्नि शिखा
206.	*Hrīmkāra Śaśi Candrikā*	ह्रींकार शशि चन्द्रिका
207.	*Hrīmkāra Bhāskara Ruciḥ*	ह्रींकार भास्कर रुचिः
208.	*Hrīmkārāmbhoda Cañcalā*	ह्रींकारांभोद चञ्चला
209.	*Hrīmkāra Kandāṅkurikā*	ह्रींकार कन्दाङ्कुरिका
210.	*Hrīmkāraika Parāyaṇā*	ह्रींकारैक परायणा
211.	*Hrīmkāra Dīrghikām Hasī*	ह्रींकार दीर्घिकां हसी
212.	*Hrīmkārodyāna Kekinī*	ह्रींकारोद्यान केकिनी

213.	*Hrīmkārāraṇya Hariṇī*	ह्रींकारारण्य हरिणी
214.	*Hrīmkārāvāla Vallarī*	ह्रींकारावाल वल्लरी
215.	*Hrīmkāra Pañjara Śukī*	ह्रींकार पञ्जर शुकी
216.	*Hrīmkārāṅgaṇa Dīpikā*	ह्रींकाराङ्गण दीपिका
217.	*Hrīmkāra Kandarāsimhī*	ह्रींकार कन्दरासिंही
218.	*Hrīmkārāmbhoja Bhruṅgikā*	ह्रींकाराम्भोज भृङ्गिका
219.	*Hrīmkāra Sumanomādhvī*	ह्रींकार सुमनोमाध्वी
220.	*Hrīmkāra Taru Mamjarī*	ह्रींकार तरु मंजरी
	Madhyakūṭam – मध्यकूटम्	
	Sa	स
221.	*Sakārākhyā*	सकाराख्या
222.	*Samarasā*	समरसा
223.	*Sakalāgama Samstutā*	सकलागम संस्तुता
224.	*Sarvavvedāntavtātparya Bhūmiḥ*	सर्वव्वेदान्तव्तात्पर्य भूमि:
225.	*Sadasadāsrayā*	सदसदास्रया
226.	*Sakalā*	सकला
227.	*Saccidānandā*	सच्चिदानन्दा
228.	*Sādhyā*	साध्या
229.	*Sadgati Dāyinī*	सद्गति दायिनी
230.	*Sanakādi Munidhyeyā*	सनकादि मुनिध्येया
231.	*Sadāśiva Kuṭumbinī*	सदाशिव कुटुम्बिनी
232.	*Sakalādhiṣṭāna Rūpā*	सकलाधिष्टान रूपा
233.	*Satya Rūpā*	सत्य रूपा
234.	*Samākrutiḥ*	समाकृति:
235.	*Sarvaprapañca Nirmātrī*	सर्वप्रपञ्च निर्मात्री
236.	*Samānādhika Varjitā*	समानाधिक वर्जिता
237.	*Sarvottuṅgā*	सर्वोत्तुङ्गा
238.	*Saṅgahīnā*	सङ्गहीना
239.	*Saguṇā*	सगुणा

240.	*Sakaleśṭadā*	सकलेश्टदा
	Ka	क
241.	*Kakāriṇī*	ककारिणी
242.	*Kāvya Lolā*	काव्य लोला
243.	*Kāmeśvara Manoharā*	कामेश्वर मनोहरा
244.	*Kāmeśvara Prāṇanāḍī*	कामेश्वर प्राणनाडी
245.	*Kāmeśotsaṅga Vāsinī*	कामेशोत्सङ्ग वासिनी
246.	*Kāmeśvarā Liṅgatāṅgī*	कामेश्वरालिङ्गताङ्गी
247.	*Kāmeśvara Sukhapradā*	कामेश्वर सुखप्रदा
248.	*Kāmeśvara Praṇayinī*	कामेश्वर प्रणयिनी
249.	*Kāmeśvara Vilāsinī*	कामेश्वर विलासिनी
250.	*Kāmeśvara Tapaḥ Siddhiḥ*	कामेश्वर तप: सिद्धि:
251.	*Kāmeśvara Manaḥ Priyā*	कामेश्वर मन: प्रिया
252.	*Kāmeśvara Prāṇa Nāthā*	कामेश्वर प्राण नाथा
253.	*Kāmeśvara Vimohinī*	कामेश्वर विमोहिनी
254.	*Kāmeśvara Brahma Vidyā*	कामेश्वर ब्रह्म विद्या
255.	*Kāmeśvara Gruheśvarī*	कामेश्वर गृहेश्वरी
256.	*Kāmeśvara Āhlādakarī*	कामेश्वर आह्लादकरी
257.	*Kāmeśvara Maheśvarī*	कामेश्वर महेश्वरी
258.	*Kāmeśvarī*	कामेश्वरी
259.	*Kāmakoṭi Nilayā*	कामकोटि निलया
260.	*Kāṅkṣitārthadā*	काङ्क्षितार्थदा
	La	ल
261.	*Lakāriṇī*	लकारिणी
262.	*Labdha Rūpā*	लब्ध रूपा
263.	*Labdhadhī*	लब्धधी
264.	*Labdha Vāñcitā*	लब्ध वाञ्चिता
265.	*Labdapāpa Manodūrā*	लब्दपाप मनोदूरा

266.	*Labdhāhamkāra Durgamā*	लब्धाहंकार दुर्गमा
267.	*Labdha Śaktiḥ*	लब्ध शक्ति:
268.	*Labdha Dehā*	लब्ध देहा
269.	*Labdhaiśvarya Samunnatiḥ*	लब्धैश्वर्य समुन्नति:
270.	*Labdha Vruddhiḥ*	लब्ध वृद्धि:
271.	*Labdha Līlā*	लब्ध लीला
272.	*Labdha Youvana Śālinī*	लब्ध यौवन शालिनी
273.	*Labdhātiśaya Sarvāṅga Soundaryā*	लब्धातिशय सर्वाङ्ग सौन्दर्या
274.	*Labdha Vibhramā*	लब्ध विभ्रमा
275.	*Labdha Rāgā*	लब्ध रागा
276.	*Labdha Patiḥ*	लब्ध पति:
277.	*Labdha Nānāgama Sthitiḥ*	लब्ध नानागम स्थिति:
278.	*Labdha Bhogā*	लब्ध भोगा
279.	*Labdha Sukhā*	लब्ध सुखा
280.	*Labdha Harśābhi Pūritā*	लब्ध हर्शाभि पूरिता
	Hrīm	ह्रीं
281.	*Hrīmkāra Mūrtiḥ*	ह्रींकार मूर्ति:
282.	*Hrīmkāra Soudha Śruṅga Kapotikā*	ह्रींकार सौध श्रृङ्ग कपोतिका
283.	*Hrīmkāra Dugdhābdhi Sudhā*	ह्रींकार दुग्धाब्धि सुधा
284.	*Hrīmkāra Kamalendirā*	ह्रींकार कमलेन्दिरा
285.	*Hrīmkāra Maṇi Dīpārcciḥ*	ह्रींकार मणि दीपार्च्चि:
286.	*Hrīmkāra Taruśārikā*	ह्रींकार तरुशारिका
287.	*Hrīmkāra Peṭakamaṇiḥ*	ह्रींकार पेटकमणि:
288.	*Hrīmkāra Darśa Bimbitā*	ह्रींकार दर्श बिम्बिता
289.	*Hrīmkāra Kośāsilatā*	ह्रींकार कोशासिलता
290.	*Hrīmkārasthāna Nartakī*	ह्रींकारस्थान नर्तकी
291.	*Hrīmkāra Śuktikā Muktā Maṇi*	ह्रींकार शुक्तिका मुक्ता मणि
292.	*Hrīmkāra Bodhitā*	ह्रींकार बोधिता
293.	*Hrīmkāramayasouvarṇa Stambhavidruma Putrikā*	ह्रींकारमयसौवर्ण स्तंभविद्रुम पुत्रिक

294.	*Hrīmkāra Vedopaniśad*	ह्रींकार वेदोपनिशद्
295.	*Hrīmkāradhvara Dakṣiṇā*	ह्रींकारध्वर दक्षिणा
296.	*Hrīmkāra Nandanārāma Navakalpakavallarī*	ह्रींकार नन्दनाराम नवकल्पकवल्लरी
297.	*Hrīmkāra Himavad Gaṅgā*	ह्रींकार हिमवद् गङ्गा
298.	*Hrīmkārārṇava Koustubhā*	ह्रींकारार्णव कौस्तुभा
299.	*Hrīmkāra Mantra Sarvasyā*	ह्रींकार मन्त्र सर्वस्या
300.	*Hrīmkāra Para Soukhyadā*	ह्रींकार पर सौख्यदा

*****

Annexure 2

300 names alphabetically (English);

#	Names in English	Names in Samskrutam
37.	*Edhamānaprabhā*	एधमानप्रभा
44.	*Eeddrugityavinirdeśyā*	ईदृगित्यविनिर्देश्या
51.	*Eeḍitā*	ईडिता
58.	*Eehāvirāhitā*	ईहाविराहिता
41.	*Eekārarūpā*	ईकाररूपा
49.	*Eekṣaṇasruṣṭāṇḍakoṭiḥ*	ईक्षणसृष्टाण्डकोटि:
48.	*Eekṣitrī*	ईक्षित्री
43.	*Eepsitārtha Pradāyinī*	ईप्सितार्थ प्रदायिनी
53.	*Eeśādhidevatā*	ईशाधिदेवता
46.	*Eeśānādibrahmamayī*	ईशानादिब्रह्ममयी
59.	*Eeśaśakti*	ईशशक्ति
55.	*Eeśatāṇḍavasākṣiṇī*	ईशताण्डवसाक्षिणी
60.	*Eeṣatsmitānanā*	ईषत्स्मितानना
42.	*Eeśitrī*	ईशित्री
47.	*Eeśitvādyaṣṭasiddhidā*	ईशित्वाद्यष्टसिद्धिदा
54.	*Eeśvarapreraṇakarī*	ईश्वरप्रेरणकरी
52.	*Eeśvarārdhāṅgaśarīrā*	ईश्वरार्धाङ्गशरीरा
45.	*Eeśvaratva Vidhāyinī*	ईश्वरत्व विधायिनी
50.	*Eeśvaravallabhā*	ईश्वरवल्लभा
56.	*Eeśvarotsaṅganilayā*	ईश्वरोत्सङ्गनिलया
57.	*Eetibādhā Vināśinī*	ईतिबाधाविनाशिनी
38.	*Ejadanejajjagadīśvarī*	एजदनेजज्जगदीश्वरी
27.	*Ekabhaktimadarcitā*	एकभक्तिमदर्चिता
32.	*Ekabhogā*	एकभोगा
28.	*Ekāgracitta Nirdhyātā*	एकाग्रचित्त निर्ध्याता

34.	*Ekaiśvarya Pradāyinī*	एकैश्वर्य प्रदायिनी
22.	*Ekākṣarī*	एकाक्षरी
25.	*Ekānanda Cidākrutiḥ*	एकानन्द चिदाकृति:
23.	*Ekānekākṣarākrutiḥ*	एकानेकाक्षराकृति:
36.	*Ekānta Pūjitā*	एकान्त पूजिता
40.	*Ekaprābhava Śālinī*	एकप्राभव शालिनी
21.	*Ekāra Rūpā*	एकार रूपा
33.	*Ekarasā*	एकरसा
35.	*Ekātapatra Sāmrājyapradā*	एकातपत्र साम्राज्यप्रदा
39.	*Ekavīrādi Samsevyā*	एकवीरादि संसेव्या
30.	*Elāsugamdhi Cikurā*	एलासुगंधि चिकुरा
31.	*Enaḥ Kūṭa Vināśinī*	एन:कूट विनाशिनी
29.	*Eṣaṇā Rahitāddhrutā*	एषणा रहिताद्धृता
24.	*Etattaditya Nirdeśyā*	एतत्तदित्य निर्देश्या
26.	*Evamityāgamābodhyā*	एवमित्यागमाबोध्या
119.	*Hādividyā*	हादिविद्या
177.	*Hāhā Hūhū Mukhastutyā*	हाहा हूहू मुखस्तुत्या
161.	*Hakārārthā*	हकारार्था
101.	*Hakārarūpā*	हकाररूपा
165.	*Hākinī*	हाकिनी
102.	*Haladhrutpūjitā*	हलधृत्पूजिता
120.	*Hālāmadālasā*	हालामदालसा
172.	*Hallīsalāsya Santuṣṭā*	हल्लीसलास्य सन्तुष्टा
166.	*Halyavarjitā*	हल्यवर्जिता
162.	*Hamsa Gatiḥ*	हंस गति:
173.	*Hamsa Mantrārthā Rūpiṇī*	हंस मन्त्रार्था रूपिणी
110.	*Hamsavāhanā*	हंसवाहना
178.	*Hāni Vruddhi Vivarjitā*	हानि वृद्धि विवर्जिता

174.	*Hānopādāna Nirmuktā*	हानोपादान निर्मुक्ता
164.	*Hāraharikucābhogā*	हारहरिकुचाभोगा
105.	*Harārādhyā*	हराराध्या
171.	*Hārda Santamasāpahā*	हार्द सन्तमसापहा
176.	*Hari Sodarī*	हरि सोदरी
106.	*Haribrahmendra Vanditā*	हरिब्रह्मेन्द्र वन्दिता
113.	*Haridaśvādi Sevitā*	हरिदश्वादि सेविता
116.	*Haridrākuṅkumādigdhā*	हरिद्राकुङ्कुमादिग्धा
180.	*Harigopāruṇāmśukā*	हरिगोपारुणांशुका
103.	*Hariṇekṣṇā*	हरिणेक्ष्णा
104.	*Haripriyā*	हरिप्रिया
167.	*Haritpati Samārādhyā*	हरित्पति समाराध्या
118.	*Harkeśasakhī*	हर्केशसखी
169.	*Harṣapradā*	हर्षप्रदा
175.	*Harṣiṇī*	हर्षिणी
109.	*Haryakṣavāhanā*	हर्यक्षवाहना
117.	*Haryaśvādyamarārcitā*	हर्यश्वाद्यमरार्चिता
115.	*Hastikruttipriyāṅganā*	हस्तिकृत्तिप्रियाङ्गना
114.	*Hastikumbhottuṅkakucā*	हस्तिकुम्भोत्तुङ्ककुचा
111.	*Hatadānavā*	हतदानवा
163.	*Hāṭakābharaṇojvalā*	हाटकाभरणोज्वला
168.	*Haṭhātkāra Hatāsurā*	हठात्कार हतासुरा
112.	*Hatyādi Pāpaśamanī*	हत्यादि पापशमनी
170.	*Havirbhoktrī*	हविर्भोक्त्री
108.	*Hayamedhasamarcitā*	हयमेधसमर्चिता
107.	*Hayārūḍhāsevitāmghriḥ*	हयारूढासेवितांघ्रिः
179.	*Hayyaṅgavīna Hrudayā*	हय्यङ्गवीन हृदया
99.	*Hrīm*	ह्रीं
92.	*Hrīm Garbhā*	ह्रीं गर्भा

100.	*Hrīm Śarīriṇī*	ह्रीं शरीरेणी
90.	*Hrīm Śīlā*	ह्रीं शीला
89.	*Hrīm Vibhūṣaṇā*	ह्रीं विभूषणा
84.	*Hrīmkāra Bījā*	ह्रींकार बीजा
207.	*Hrīmkāra Bhāskara Ruciḥ*	ह्रींकार भास्कर रुचि:
292.	*Hrīmkāra Bodhitā*	ह्रींकार बोधिता
98.	*Hrīmkāra Cintyā*	ह्रींकार चिन्त्या
288.	*Hrīmkāra Darśa Bimbitā*	ह्रींकार दर्श बिम्बिता
211.	*Hrīmkāra Dīrghikām Hasī*	ह्रींकार दीर्घिकां हसी
283.	*Hrīmkāra Dugdhābdhi Sudhā*	ह्रींकार दुग्धाब्धि सुधा
297.	*Hrīmkāra Himavad Gaṅgā*	ह्रींकार हिमवद् गङ्गा
87.	*Hrīmkāra Japasuprītā*	ह्रींकार जपसुप्रीता
284.	*Hrīmkāra Kamalendirā*	ह्रींकार कमलेन्दिरा
209.	*Hrīmkāra Kandāṅkurikā*	ह्रींकार कन्दाङ्कुरिका
217.	*Hrīmkāra Kandarāsimhī*	ह्रींकार कन्दरासिंही
289.	*Hrīmkāra Kośāsilatā*	ह्रींकार कोशासिलता
205.	*Hrīmkāra Kuṇḍāgni Śikhā*	ह्रींकार कुण्डाग्नि शिखा
86.	*Hrīmkāra Lakṣaṇā*	ह्रींकार लक्षणा
285.	*Hrīmkāra Maṇi Dīpārcciḥ*	ह्रींकार मणि दीपार्च्चि:
85.	*Hrīmkāra Mantrā*	ह्रींकार मन्त्रा
299.	*Hrīmkāra Mantra Sarvasyā*	ह्रींकार मन्त्र सर्वस्या
281.	*Hrīmkāra Mūrtiḥ*	ह्रींकार मूर्ति:
296.	*Hrīmkāra Nandanārāma Navakalpakavallarī*	ह्रींकार नन्दनाराम नवकल्पकवल्लरी
82.	*Hrīmkāra Nilayā*	ह्रींकार निलया
215.	*Hrīmkāra Pañjara Śukī*	ह्रींकार पञ्जर शुकी
300.	*Hrīmkāra Para Soukhyadā*	ह्रींकार पर सौख्यदा
96.	*Hrīmkāra Pīṭhikā*	ह्रींकार पीठिका
287.	*Hrīmkāra Peṭakamaṇiḥ*	ह्रींकार पेटकमणि:

95.	*Hrīmkāra Pūjyā*	ह्रींकार पूज्या
81.	*Hrīmkāra Rūpā*	ह्रींकार रूपा
206.	*Hrīmkāra Śaśi Candrikā*	ह्रींकार शशि चन्द्रिका
282.	*Hrīmkāra Soudha Śruṅga Kapotikā*	ह्रींकार सौध श्रृङ्ग कपोतिका
291.	*Hrīmkāra Śuktikā Muktā Maṇi*	ह्रींकार शुक्तिका मुक्ता मणि
219.	*Hrīmkāra Sumanomādhvī*	ह्रींकार सुमनोमाध्वी
220.	*Hrīmkāra Taru Mamjarī*	ह्रींकार तरु मंजरी
286.	*Hrīmkāra Taruśārikā*	ह्रींकार तरुशारिका
94.	*Hrīmkāra Vācyā*	ह्रींकार वाच्या
294.	*Hrīmkāra Vedopaniśad*	ह्रींकार वेदोपनिशद्
97.	*Hrīmkāra Vedyā*	ह्रींकार वेद्या
295.	*Hrīmkāradhvara Dakṣiṇā*	ह्रींकारध्वर दक्षिणा
202.	*Hrīmkārādiḥ*	ह्रींकारादि:
210.	*Hrīmkāraika Parāyaṇā*	ह्रींकारैक परायणा
293.	*Hrīmkāramayasouvarṇa Stambhavidruma Putrikā*	ह्रींकारमयसौवर्ण स्तंभविद्रुम पुत्रिका
208.	*Hrīmkārāmbhoda Cañcalā*	ह्रींकारांभोद चञ्चला
218.	*Hrīmkārāmbhoja Bhruṅgikā*	ह्रींकाराम्भोज भृङ्गिका
216.	*Hrīmkārāṅgaṇa Dīpikā*	ह्रींकाराङ्गण दीपिका
213.	*Hrīmkārāraṇya Hariṇī*	ह्रींकारारण्य हरिणी
298.	*Hrīmkārārṇava Koustubhā*	ह्रींकारार्णव कौस्तुभा
290.	*Hrīmkārasthāna Nartakī*	ह्रींकारस्थान नर्तकी
214.	*Hrīmkārāvāla Vallarī*	ह्रींकारावाल वल्लरी
201.	*Hrīmkāriṇī*	ह्रींकारिणी
212.	*Hrīmkārodyāna Kekinī*	ह्रींकारोद्यान केकिनी
203.	*Hrīmmadhyā*	ह्रींमध्या
88.	*Hrīmmatiḥ*	ह्रींमति:
93.	*Hrīmpadābhidhā*	ह्रींपदाभिधा
83.	*Hrīmpadapriyā*	ह्रींपदप्रिया

91.	*Hrīmpadārādhyā*	ह्रींपदाराध्या
204.	*Hrīmśikhāmaṇiḥ*	ह्रींशिखामणि:
150.	*Kacajitāmbhudā*	कचजिताम्भुदा
11.	*Kadamba Kusumapriyā*	कदम्ब कुसुमप्रिया
10.	*Kadambakānana Vāsā*	कदम्बकानन वासा
141.	*Kakārārthā*	ककारार्था
1.	*Kakārarūpā*	ककाररूपा
241.	*Kakāriṇī*	ककारिणी
142.	*Kālahantrī*	कालहन्त्री
156.	*Kalālāpā*	कलालापा
149.	*Kalānāthamukhī*	कलानाथमुखी
6.	*Kalāvatī*	कलावती
15.	*Kalidoṣaharā*	कलिदोषहरा
8.	*Kalmaṣaghnī*	कल्मषघ्नी
159.	*Kalpavallīsamabhujā*	कल्पवल्लीसमभुजा
146.	*Kalyā*	कल्या
3.	*Kalyāṇa Guṇaśālinī*	कल्याण गुणशालिनी
4.	*Kalyāṇa Śailanilayā*	कल्याण शैलनिलया
2.	*Kalyāṇī*	कल्याणी
259.	*Kāmakoṭi Nilayā*	कामकोटि निलया
7.	*Kamalākṣī*	कमलाक्षी
5.	*Kamanīyā*	कमनीया
145.	*Kāmasañjīvinī*	कामसञ्जीविनी
157.	*Kambukaṇṭhī*	कम्बुकण्ठी
143.	*Kāmeśī*	कामेशी
245.	*Kāmeśotsaṅga Vāsinī*	कामेशोत्सङ्ग वासिनी
256.	*Kāmeśvara Āhlādakarī*	कामेश्वर आह्लादकरी
254.	*Kāmeśvara Brahma Vidyā*	कामेश्वर ब्रह्म विद्या

255.	*Kāmeśvara Gruheśvarī*	कामेश्वर गृहेश्वरी
257.	*Kāmeśvara Maheśvarī*	कामेश्वर महेश्वरी
251.	*Kāmeśvara Manaḥ Priyā*	कामेश्वर मन: प्रिया
243.	*Kāmeśvara Manoharā*	कामेश्वर मनोहरा
252.	*Kāmeśvara Prāṇa Nāthā*	कामेश्वर प्राण नाथा
244.	*Kāmeśvara Prāṇanāḍī*	कामेश्वर प्राणनाडी
248.	*Kāmeśvara Praṇayinī*	कामेश्वर प्रणयिनी
247.	*Kāmeśvara Sukhapradā*	कामेश्वर सुखप्रदा
250.	*Kāmeśvara Tapaḥ Siddhiḥ*	कामेश्वर तप: सिद्धि:
249.	*Kāmeśvara Vilāsinī*	कामेश्वर विलासिनी
253.	*Kāmeśvara Vimohinī*	कामेश्वर विमोहिनी
246.	*Kāmeśvarāliṅgatāṅgī*	कामेश्वरालिङ्गताङ्गी
258.	*Kāmeśvarī*	कामेश्वरी
144.	*Kāmitārthadā*	कामितार्थदा
17.	*Kamravigrahā*	कम्रविग्रहा
13.	*Kandarpa Janakāpāṅga Vīkṣaṇā*	कन्दर्प जनकापाङ्ग वीक्षणा
12.	*Kandarpa Vidhyā*	कन्दर्प विध्या
16.	*Kaṅjalocanā*	कञ्जलोचना
260.	*Kāṅkṣitārthadā*	काङ्क्षितार्थदा
154.	*Kāntā*	कान्ता
155.	*Kāntidhūtajapāvaliḥ*	कान्तिधूतजपावलि:
152.	*Kapāliprāṇanāyikā*	कपालिप्राणनायिका
148.	*Karabhoruḥ*	करभोरु:
158.	*Karanirjitapallavā*	करनिर्जितपल्लवा
19.	*Kārayitrī*	कारयित्री
18.	*Karmādi Sākṣiṇī*	कर्मादि साक्षिणी
20.	*Karmaphalapradā*	कर्मफलप्रदा
14.	*Karpūravīṭi Sourabhya Kallolita Kakuptaṭā*	कर्पूरवीटि सौरभ्य कल्लोलित ककुप्तटा

9.	*Karuṇāmruta Sāgarā*	करुणामृत सागरा
153.	*Kāruṇyavigrahā*	कारुण्यविग्रहा
160.	*Kastūritilakāñcitā*	कस्तूरितिलकाञ्चिता
151.	*Kaṭākṣasyandi Karuṇā*	कटाक्षस्यन्दि करुणा
147.	*Kaṭhinastana Maṇḍalā*	कठिनस्तन मण्डला
242.	*Kāvya Lolā*	काव्य लोला
265.	*Labdapāpa Manodūrā*	लब्दपाप मनोदूरा
192.	*Labdha Bhakti Sulabhā*	लब्ध भक्ति सुलभा
278.	*Labdha Bhogā*	लब्ध भोगा
268.	*Labdha Dehā*	लब्ध देहा
280.	*Labdha Harśābhi Pūritā*	लब्ध हर्शाभि पूरिता
271.	*Labdha Līlā*	लब्ध लीला
277.	*Labdha Nānāgama Sthitiḥ*	लब्ध नानागम स्थिति:
276.	*Labdha Patiḥ*	लब्ध पति:
275.	*Labdha Rāgā*	लब्ध रागा
262.	*Labdha Rūpā*	लब्ध रूपा
267.	*Labdha Śaktiḥ*	लब्ध शक्ति:
200.	*Labdha Sampat Samunnatiḥ*	लब्ध संपत् समुन्नति:
279.	*Labdha Sukhā*	लब्ध सुखा
264.	*Labdha Vāṅcitā*	लब्ध वाञ्चिता
274.	*Labdha Vibhramā*	लब्ध विभ्रमा
270.	*Labdha Vruddhiḥ*	लब्ध वृद्धि:
272.	*Labdha Youvana Śālinī*	लब्ध यौवन शालिनी
263.	*Labdhadhī*	लब्धधी
266.	*Labdhāhamkāra Durgamā*	लब्धाहंकार दुर्गमा
269.	*Labdhaiśvarya Samunnatiḥ*	लब्धैश्वर्य समुन्नति:
73.	*Labdhakāmā*	लब्धकामा
198.	*Labdhamānā*	लब्धमाना

199.	*Labdharasā*	लब्धरसा
273.	*Labdhātiśaya Sarvāṅga Soundaryā*	लब्धातिशय सर्वाङ्ग सौन्दर्या
185.	*Lābhālābhā Vivarjitā*	लाभालाभा विवर्जिता
78.	*Labhyā*	लभ्या
191.	*Labhyetarā*	लभ्येतरा
188.	*Laghusiddhidā*	लघुसिद्धिदा
194.	*Lagnacāmara Hasta Śrī Śāradā Parivījitā*	लग्नचामर हस्त श्री शारदा परिवीजिता
79.	*Lajjāḍhyā*	लज्जाढ्या
195.	*Lajjāpada Samārādhyā*	लज्जापद समाराध्या
181.	*Lakārākhyā*	लकाराख्या
61.	*Lakārarūpā*	लकाररूपा
261.	*Lakāriṇī*	लकारिणी
64.	*Lākinī*	लाकिनी
70.	*Lakṣakoṭyaṇḍa Nāyikā*	लक्षकोट्यण्ड नायिका
69.	*Lakṣanojjvala Divyāṅgī*	लक्षनोज्ज्वल दिव्याङ्गी
189.	*Lākṣārasasavarṇābhā*	लाक्षारससवर्णाभा
190.	*Lakṣmaṇāgraja Pūjitā*	लक्ष्मणाग्रज पूजिता
63.	*Lakṣmīvāṇī Niṣevitā*	लक्ष्मीवाणी निषेविता
72.	*Lakṣṇāgamyā*	लक्ष्णागम्या
71.	*Lakṣyārthā*	लक्ष्यार्था
197.	*Lakuleśvarī*	लकुलेश्वरी
75.	*Lalāmarājadalikā*	ललामराजदलिका
65.	*Lalanārūpā*	ललनारूपा
67.	*Lalantikā Lasatphālā*	ललन्तिका लसत्फाला
68.	*Lalāṭanayanārcitā*	ललाटनयनार्चिता
62.	*Lalitā*	ललिता
76.	*Lambimuktālatāñcitā*	लम्बिमुक्तालताञ्चिता
77.	*Lambodaraprasūḥ*	लम्बोदरप्रसूः

196.	*Lampaṭā*	लंपटा
193.	*Lāṅgalāyudhā*	लाङ्गलायुधा
186.	*Laṅghyetarāṅā*	लङ्घ्येतराज्ञा
66.	*Lasaddhāḍimapāṭalā*	लसद्धाडिमपाटला
184.	*Lāsya Darśana Santuṣṭā*	लास्य दर्शन सन्तुष्टा
182.	*Latāpūjyā*	लतापूज्या
74.	*Latātanuḥ*	लतातनु:
187.	*Lāvaṇya Śālinī*	लावण्य शालिनी
183.	*Layasthiti Udbhaveśvarī*	लयस्थिति उद्भवेश्वरी
80.	*Layavarjitā*	लयवर्जिता
238.	*Saṅgahīnā*	सङ्गहीना
227.	*Saccidānandā*	सच्चिदानन्दा
225.	*Sadasadāsrayā*	सदसदास्रया
231.	*Sadāśiva Kuṭumbinī*	सदाशिव कुटुम्बिनी
229.	*Sadgati Dāyinī*	सद्गति दायिनी
228.	*Sādhyā*	साध्या
239.	*Saguṇā*	सगुणा
226.	*Sakalā*	सकला
232.	*Sakalādhiṣṭāna Rūpā*	सकलाधिष्टान रूपा
223.	*Sakalāgama Samstutā*	सकलागम संस्तुता
240.	*Sakaleṣṭadā*	सकलेश्टदा
221.	*Sakārākhyā*	सकाराख्या
121.	*Sakārarūpā*	सकाररूपा
234.	*Samākrutiḥ*	समाकृति:
236.	*Samānādhika Varjitā*	समानाधिक वर्जिता
222.	*Samarasā*	समरसा
230.	*Sanakādi Munidhyeyā*	सनकादि मुनिध्येया
128.	*Sanātanā*	सनातना

134.	*Sarva Vimohinī*	सर्व विमोहिनी
126.	*Sarvabhartrī*	सर्वभर्त्री
140.	*Sarvabhūṣaṇabhūṣitā*	सर्वभूषणभूषिता
135.	*Sarvādhārā*	सर्वाधारा
136.	*Sarvagatā*	सर्वगता
127.	*Sarvahantrī*	सर्वहन्त्री
125.	*Sarvakartrī*	सर्वकर्त्री
124.	*Sarvamaṅgalā*	सर्वमङ्गला
139.	*Sarvamātā*	सर्वमाता
122.	*Sarvaṅā*	सर्वञा
129.	*Sarvanavadyā*	सर्वनवद्या
130.	*Sarvāṅga Sundarī*	सर्वाङ्ग सुन्दरी
235.	*Sarvaprapañca Nirmātrī*	सर्वप्रपञ्च निर्मात्री
138.	*Sarvāruṇā*	सर्वारुणा
131.	*Sarvasākṣiṇī*	सर्वसाक्षिणी
133.	*Sarvasoukhyadātrī*	सर्वसौख्यदात्री
132.	*Sarvātmikā*	सर्वात्मिका
137.	*Sarvāvaguṇavarjitā*	सर्वावगुणवर्जिता
224.	*Sarvavvedāntavtātparya Bhūmiḥ*	सर्वव्वेदान्तव्तात्पर्य भूमि:
123.	*Sarveśī*	सर्वेशी
237.	*Sarvottuṅgā*	सर्वोत्तुङ्गा
233.	*Satya Rūpā*	सत्य रूपा

About the Author

http://ramamurthy.jaagruti.co.in/

Ramamurthy is a versatile personallty having experlence and expertise in varlous

areas of Banking, related IT solutions, information Securlty, IT Audlt, Vedas, Samskruta and so on.

Hls thlrst for continuous learning does not subslde even at the age of late flfties. He is also pursuing research on information Technology and Samskruta and has submltted his dlssertation for Ph.D. degree. He is into a project of developing a Samskruta based compller.

It is his passlon to spread his knowledge and experlence through conducting classes, training programmes and wrlting books.

He has already publlshed books:

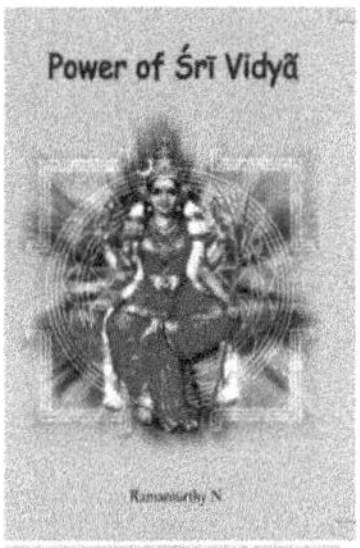

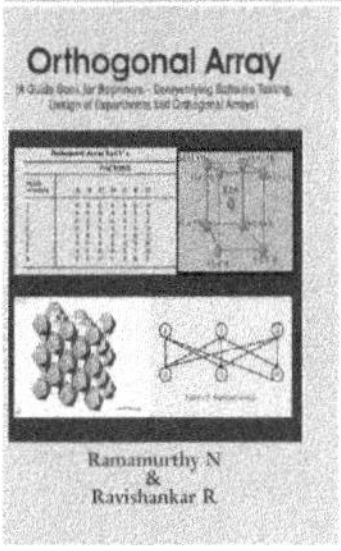

Hls other books are being publlshed:

Books being penned:

- Corporate Finance,
- Banking – GRC
- information Securlty in Banks
- And more
-

May *Śrī Devee* shower Her cholcest blessings on him and may we expect many more of such endeavours from him.

*****

Bibiliography

1. Book *"Śrī Lalitā Sahasranāmam"* – English translation of *Bhāskararāyā's bhāshyam* – by the same author
2. Book "Power of *Śrī Vidyā*" – by the same author
3. Voice of God – *Kānchi Paramāchāryā's* speeches – 7 volumes – English translation of series of books in Tamil called *"Deivathin Kural"*
4. Book *"Śrī Chakra* – An Esoteric Approach" by the same author

*****

www.ingramcontent.com/pod-product-compliance
Lightning Source LLC
Chambersburg PA
CBHW071506040426
42444CB00008B/1513
* 9 7 8 9 3 8 2 2 3 7 1 7 4 *